Belief in God

A STUDY IN THE EPISTEMOLOGY
OF RELIGION

Studies in Philosophy

ჟᲓ

CONSULTING EDITOR: *V. C. Chappell*, The University of Chicago

George I. Mavrodes

Belief in God

A STUDY IN THE EPISTEMOLOGY
OF RELIGION

 Random House   New York

Library of Congress Catalog Card Number: 78–92831

Manufactured in the United States of America. Printed
and Bound by Halliday Lithograph Corporation,
West Hanover, Mass.

TYPOGRAPHY BY JANE NORLING

FIRST PRINTING

Contents

Introduction

This book deals with a limited aspect of religion. Any well-developed religion is a very complex entity which unites components of very different sorts. There is probably no living religion that does not involve a set of characteristic beliefs, some prescribed or recommended practices (public or private, or both), some characteristic feelings or emotions, and some institutions or social arrangements. In addition, religions usually involve their adherents in special forms of experience. With respect to the complexity that it generates, interest in religion is similar to other pervasive human interests and activities, such as those that generate scientific enterprises.* For some purposes, however, it is useful to separate the aspects of a complex phenomenon and to discuss one or another of these aspects individually, so far as is possible. This is the procedure that I will adopt here. My discussion is aimed primarily at that element of religious interest that centers upon

* For an interesting comparison between religion and science, especially with respect to the role of institutions and sociological factors see William G. Pollard, *Physicist and Christian* (New York: The Seaburg Press, 1961).

belief, with what one might call the *noetic* aspect of religion. Some of the other aspects that I have mentioned—most notably religious experience and, to a much smaller extent, religious institutions—are discussed, but only to the extent that I take them to be relevant to questions about belief. But, of course, this should not be construed to imply that these other aspects of religion are unimportant.

Even with respect to belief, however, my discussion will not be exhaustive. For many religious beliefs—indeed, for many of those in which I am most interested—I think the most important question that one can ask is "Is it true?" But I will not have very much to say directly about the truth of these beliefs. This is in spite of the fact that I have strong convictions about the truth of certain religious beliefs, and also in spite of the fact that I have no special reason to conceal those convictions.* I do not deal directly with the truth of religious beliefs because I think that such a discussion is likely to be fruitful only if it can be done in a special way and under special circumstances. My reason for thinking this will become clearer, I hope, in the course of the discussion. What I hope to do is to carry out an investigation that is now, for many people, a required preliminary to usefully engaging themselves in the question of the truth of religious beliefs. But it is only preliminary and so it would be unfortunate if one's intellectual excursion into the realm of religion were to end where this book ends. I would hope, rather, that this discussion will serve as an aid to those who wish to investigate for themselves or perhaps to discuss with others, in the appropriate circumstances, the great questions of religious truth.

The topic that I will deal with is religious *epistemology.* Roughly, we might say that epistemological interests are those that are reflected by questions such as "How do you know that *p*?" and "What are your reasons for believing that *p*?" In Chapter I these questions are discussed somewhat more in detail and some groundwork is laid for the subsequent dis-

* To allay the possible curiosity of some readers, I do not mind saying that I accept Protestant Christianity of a fairly orthodox or evangelical variety.

cussion. Chapter II deals with attempts to answer such questions when they involve religious beliefs, by reference to arguments, especially proofs of God's existence. This chapter is probably longer than the intrinsic importance of argumentation in religious contexts would justify. It is convenient, however, to make some more general points in connection with a discussion of argumentation and then to extend them to other contexts. Chapter III discusses the alternative attempt to answer the epistemological questions in terms of experience and—as a special type of experience—revelation. Chapter IV deals with the epistemological aspects of the problem of evil, which is often elaborated as a proof against certain religious doctrines. Chapter V provides a recapitulation of the main thread of the argument and its most important consequences.

Belief in God

Epistemological Questions

Epistemological questions are primarily concerned with the sources of knowledge and with the reasons for belief. In this chapter I will make some preliminary observations on these topics, observations that hopefully will be sufficient to enable us to proceed with the remainder of the argument. The chapter is divided into three sections: Section (1) discusses very briefly the notion of knowledge; Section (2) deals with questions of the form "How do you know that p?" and calls attention to an important ambiguity which they conceal; Section (3) discusses some of the possible relations between having a reason and giving a reason for one's beliefs.

1 ↝ Knowing

THE PROPOSITIONAL SENSE. Throughout this book I will have occasion to use the verb "to know." I will use it primarily in its propositional sense, that is, the sense in which it applies to some proposition or statement, to some set of propositions, or to some generalization over propositions. We can identify the propositional sense in sentences of the form "N knows that p" where N is to be replaced by the name or description of some person or persons (or some generalization over persons) and p is to be replaced by the expression for some proposition or propositions (or some generalization over propositions). The following are examples of sentences that have this form:

Professor Plushbottom knows that his class will not meet today.

All of us here know that what the chairman said is false.

No one knows anything about the origin of quasars.

There are other meanings of "to know." One of these is that of "knowing how" as in "All Boy Scouts know how to build a campfire." Another important use is in instances where the verb takes as its object the name or description of some person, as in "I know Patrick Flanagan very well." Although there are interesting relations between these senses and the propositional sense, the latter meaning is the only one that we shall have occasion to use or discuss.

KNOWING AND BELIEVING. In the sense in which I shall use these terms, a statement of the form "N knows that p" will logically entail "N believes that p." In other words, the claim that N *knows* a certain proposition cannot be true unless it is also true that N *believes* that proposition. (The converse entailment, however, from believing to knowing, does not hold.)

I will not attempt to define the verb "to believe" beyond saying that it refers to a certain type of psychological state, attitude, or disposition directed toward or involving a certain proposition. The reader is no doubt already sufficiently familiar with this term to follow the remainder of this discussion without difficulty.

KNOWING AND TRUTH. As I shall use these terms, a proposition of the form "*N* knows that *p*" will logically entail "*p* is true." In other words, the claim that someone knows a certain proposition cannot be true unless the proposition that is said to be known is also true.

This is one of the contrasts between belief and knowledge. A person may truly be said to *believe p*, even if *p* is in fact false. But he cannot truly be said to know *p* if *p* is in fact false. The concept of knowledge may therefore be said to include the notion of belief plus some additional elements, one of which is truth.

Just as with the verb to know, I will use the adjective "true" exclusively in its propositional sense—the sense that it has when it modifies or is predicated of propositions or statements. When used in this sense, a proposition of the form "*p* is true" is logically equivalent to *p*. In other words, a given proposition is true if and only if the state of affairs that the proposition asserts to be the case is actually the case. And a proposition will be false if and only if it is not true. So the proposition "God exists" is true just in case there is a God, and if there is no God then the proposition is false.

Notice that the foregoing analysis is an account of the *meaning* of "true," and not a recipe for finding out whether a given proposition is, in fact, true. And so it provides us with a procedure for discovering truth only in the most general sense. One may be presented with a proposition such as "The capsules in this bottle contain quinine" and may wish to determine whether this proposition is true. According to this definition of "true" we are informed that in order to determine whether the proposition is true we must discover whether the capsules contain quinine. But it does not tell us *how* to make this latter discovery. Presumably, a pharmacologist may be able to teach us one method. But neither the pharmacological method nor any other method of determining the presence of quinine is a part of the meaning of "true."[1]

KNOWING AND REASONS. Philosophers often claim that there is another difference between knowledge and belief—a difference that is related to having "reasons." A person may truly be said to believe *p* regardless of what reason he may have for *p* and, indeed, regardless of whether he has any reason at all. He cannot, however, be said to know *p* unless he has some good reason. So a proposition of the form "*N* knows that *p*" entails "*N* has some good reason for believing that *p*." Although we might be inclined to agree with this observation, it seems difficult to formulate a definition of a "good reason" that is both general (it applies to all cases) and informative. It is perhaps easier to make some progress by discussing particular cases. That is, although we may not be very confident of how to characterize good reasons in general, there may be particular situations in which we may be sure that a person does or does not have a good reason for what he believes. Much of the remainder of this book is concerned with reasons for and against belief in God.

2 ⊷ How Do You Know?

Questions of the form "How do you know that *p*?" and the closely related "What reason do you have for believing that *p*?" often occur in discussions of religious belief. These questions often seem inordinately difficult to answer and can signal the end of useful discussion. This may be due in part to an important ambiguity which the expression "How do you know?" conceals. While the distinction that is involved in this ambiguity will be discussed in Chapters II and III, it may be useful to give a preliminary account of it here.

THE SOURCE OF THE AMBIGUITY. Imagine a girl who has gone to considerable trouble to keep her engagement a secret from everyone except her immediate family and that of her fiancé. She is then disconcerted when a casual acquaintance

relevantly to the challenge, even if he says nothing about himself: if he convinces the atheist that God exists, he will have met that challenge successfully.

This brings us to another feature of the challenge which again contrasts with the biographical question. Responses to the challenge may perhaps be evaluated in terms of their truth or falsity. But it is also important to evaluate these responses in terms of their effectiveness or success. The challenge poses a task, and therefore it seems relevant to evaluate the responses in terms of their success or potential for success in that task. It is not at all clear, however, that such criteria have any relevance to the biographical question or to its answer: that question simply demands a certain piece of information and relevant answers will either provide that information or substitute for it some falsehood. Here the categories of truth and falsity seem sufficient for the evaluation of responses.

This point suggests still another contrast. It is difficult to imagine a relevant response to the biographical question that does not involve saying (or writing) something. A piece of information has been requested and the standard way to provide it is by linguistic means—by making further statements or explanations. For challenges, however, it is by no means clear that the most relevant or even the most standard response must be in words. In general, we can notice that nonverbal means are often the most effective and the most appropriate for convincing a person of the truth of some proposition. Thus, the driver convinces the police officer that he has a license not by talking but by drawing the license from his wallet and exhibiting it. Similarly, the lawyer convinces the jury partly by his speech but also in part by exhibiting weapons and fingerprints. We should therefore keep in mind that in the religious context as well, the best response to some questions of the challenge type may not be entirely verbal.

KANT'S QUESTIONS. It may be interesting to note that this ambiguity infects a famous series of questions asked by Immanuel Kant. His *Prolegomena to any Future Metaphysics* is built around four questions:

(1) How is pure mathematics possible?
(2) How is pure natural science possible?
(3) How is pure metaphysics in general possible?
(4) How is metaphysics as a science possible?[2]

Kant considered all of these questions important and devoted a great deal of work to each one. At first sight the questions seem to be basically similar—that is, they seem to ask the same thing about several different human enterprises. But we may begin to suspect that they are not so similar when we find Kant portentously announcing that "all metaphysicians are therefore solemnly and legally suspended from their occupations till they shall have answered in a satisfactory manner the question, 'How are synthetic cognitions *a priori* possible?' "[3] For he did not suspend the mathematicians and the natural scientists from their accustomed tasks until they had answered the corresponding questions about their activities. Why not?

Kant's reason for treating the metaphysicians so differently from the mathematicians and the scientists is not that he thought these latter thinkers had already answered these questions. He apparently believed that he himself was the first to give the true account of how mathematics and natural science were possible. But we are provided with an insight into the reason for this differential treatment when we find Kant beginning his discussion of the question about mathematics with the statement:

> Here is a great and established branch of knowledge, encompassing even now a wonderfully large domain and promising an unlimited extension in the future. Yet it carries with it thoroughly apodeictical certainty, i.e., absolute necessity, which therefore rests upon no empirical grounds.[4]

Given that we have such knowledge, he then asks how we could have come to have it. In a similar way he writes of natural science:

> We nevertheless actually possess a pure science of nature in which are propounded, *a priori* with all the necessity requisite to apodeictical propositions, laws to which nature is subject. . . . There is then in fact a pure science of nature, and the question arises, *How is it possible?*[5]

He thus has no doubt that there are pure sciences of mathematics and nature and that, by means of them, truths are being brought to knowledge. For mathematics and science, then, his "How" questions express no doubt about the truth of the propositions that are claimed as known. Kant takes that truth for granted.

    Nowhere, however, does he say similar things about metaphysics. He apparently did not believe that any genuine metaphysics was already in existence nor that the propositions commonly put forward by metaphysicians constituted a well-founded body of truths. Consequently, his "How" questions about metaphysics, though superficially similar to the others, really express a quite different doubt—the doubt as to whether metaphysics is even possible. Once we understand the different sense that these questions have, Kant's differential treatment of the metaphysicians no longer seems puzzling.

3 ᵉᔆ *Having a Reason and Giving a Reason*

In Section (1) I said that knowing may require having a reason. There is some temptation to convert this statement into the requirement that one should give—or perhaps be able to give—a reason. But it is not at all clear that "having a reason" must mean "being able to give a reason" and it might be wise not to commit ourselves too early to some rigid connection between the two.

HAVING AND GIVING. Suppose that someone asks us whether we *have* a reason for some particular belief and also whether we can *give* a reason for that belief. Abstractly, there seem to be four possibilities:

(a) We have reasons and we can give reasons.
(b) We have reasons but we cannot give any.
(c) We have no reasons but we can give some.
(d) We have no reasons and we cannot give any.

At first sight (a) and (d) may seem to be the only genuine possibilities, with (b) and (c) being absurd. If we have reasons, it might be asked, why should it not be possible to give them? And perhaps (c) is even worse than (b) for how can we give something that we do not have? But if (a) and (d) are the only real possibilities, then it will be the case that we can *give* a reason whenever we *have* a reason and vice versa. If this view were correct, then no harm would be done if we insisted that knowing requires being able to give a reason as well as having a reason.

In spite of the apparent plausibility of this line of reasoning, we may be too hasty in accepting it. Its credibility is derived from the relation between having and giving in certain common cases but it overlooks the quite different relations that can arise between them in other cases.

If I have an apple then I can give an apple to a friend and if I have no apple then I cannot give one to a friend. For apples, then, the analogues of (a) and (d) seem to be the real possibilities and the analogues of (b) and (c) are absurd or impossible. But is having a reason and giving a reason like having an apple and giving an apple? Notice that if I have just one apple and I give that apple to a friend, then I will have no apple at all. Suppose that I have just one reason for my belief and I give that reason to a friend, will it follow that I will then have no reason at all for my belief? If not, then reasons are not exactly like apples, so far as having them and giving them are concerned.

Once we notice that the relations between having and giving are not exactly the same for reasons as for apples, we will be able to think of many other cases in which these relations are widely different. It certainly seems possible, for example, for a person to have a good reputation without his being able to give someone else a good reputation. The same thing also seems to be true of having a headache, a flair for music, and a premonition of disaster. No doubt we could extend this list substantially if we wished. For things of this sort, the analogue of possibility (b) is not absurd but rather very likely to be true. All of these are things that a person could have without being able to give them. Certainly having a reason is not exactly like having a headache or a good reputation, but we have already seen that neither is it like having an apple. We should therefore not be too quick to assume that it is impossible to have a reason without being able to give one.

There seem also to be some things for which the analogue of (c) is true. I may, for example, succeed in giving someone an incentive to study even if I myself have no incentive to study. And I may also be able to give someone a headache or a deep sense of insecurity without having these things myself. So not even (c) is intrinsically absurd as a statement about the possible relations between having and giving.

In the case of reasons, then, it is unwise to assume that the relations between having and giving are just those represented by (a) and (d). In fact, it is equally unwise to assume that the relations between having and giving must be the same for all reasons. Some reasons, after all, may be quite different from others; and therefore the relations between having and giving may also differ. A resolution of these uncertainties probably requires a more detailed analysis of the structure of specific types of reasons. A study of the reasons involved in argument and experience is presented in Chapters II and III.

GIVING "MY" REASON. Suppose it is true that knowing requires having a reason. Suppose also that I know a certain proposition *p*. It thus follows that I must *have* at least one reason for believing *p*. Suppose also that I am able to *give* a reason for *p*. In this case, possibility (a) is fulfilled. Does it follow that the reason which I am able to give is identical with the reason that I have? In the case of apples, of course, what I give will be identical with something that I had before the giving. But I may have a headache or an incentive to study and I may give someone else a headache or an incentive without those headaches or incentives being identical (either numerically or qualitatively). So even for cases in which (a) is fulfilled, it seems rash to assume that the reasons involved must be identical.

This observation is relevant to the discussion of challenges and their appropriate responses in Section (2). A person who receives a challenge of this sort and who really does know the proposition involved may attempt to give *his* reason. That is, he will attempt to give the reason that is related to his own belief in whatever way is required to qualify his belief as knowledge. But perhaps this way of responding to the challenge will fail in one way or other. It may be that the person has a reason that cannot by its very nature be given to another. Or though it is possible to give the reason, the person may be unsuccessful in doing so. Or it may be that he actually does give his reason but fails to convince the questioner. In any of these cases the response—regardless of what other virtues it may have—fails to be effective in meeting the challenge that is posed.

We have already recognized, however, that it may sometimes be possible for one to give a reason that is not *his* reason—in the sense that it does not bear the required relation to his own belief. If this is correct, then it may also be the case that in some circumstances giving that reason would be a more effective response to the challenge than giving one's own reason. Furthermore, this reason may have all of the other virtues that one's own reason possesses. In such a case, it would be unfortunate and unnecessary if one were to restrict his responses to his own reasons, instead of availing himself of this wider range of possible responses.

GIVING AND RECEIVING. Two last questions should be raised here. If I give someone a reason for believing *p*, does it follow that he then has a reason for believing *p*? And if he does have a reason after I give him one—though he had none before—does it follow that the reason that he now has is identical with the reason that I gave him? Or may it be quite different?

Regarding the first question, we may notice that some people apparently believe that one can sometimes give a reason (perhaps one's own reason) by talking. It is possible, however, for a person to talk and for everything that he says to be true and relevant, without his being believed by his hearers. Suppose, then, that I believe *p* and that there is some reason for *p* that I can give by talking. And suppose that I speak to someone who does not believe *p* and who has no reason to believe *p* and I give him this reason. Then suppose that he does not believe what I say when I give him that reason. It is hard to see in what sense that person has any more reason to believe *p* than he had before, merely because he has heard something else that he does not believe.

With respect to the second question, we might consider the following case. I see an auto accident at the corner of State and Liberty streets, and consequently I believe that there has been an accident there. I express this belief to someone who has no reason to believe that there has been such an accident, and he asks how I know, or what my reason is. Apparently, some people believe that I can give my reason by saying "I saw it myself." At any rate, it certainly seems to be the case that by saying this I report or tell him what my reason is. Perhaps my hearer believes me to be a careful observer and a man of good character and so perhaps he comes to have a reason for believing that there was such an accident. But it is clear that the reason that he has is not identical or even very similar to my reason. For his reason seems to involve my report or testimony in a way in which mine does not (notice that whether I am of good character is relevant to *his* having a good reason but not to *my* having a good reason).

NOTES

1. Readers who are interested in a further discussion of the notion of truth will find a very stimulating set of papers by recent and contemporary philosophers in George Pitcher (ed.), *Truth* (Englewood Cliffs, New Jersey: Prentice-Hall, 1964). That volume also contains a valuable bibliography of other published work on this topic.
2. Immanuel Kant, *Prolegomena to any Future Metaphysics,* tr. Paul Carus (Chicago: The Open Court Publishing Company, 1929), p. 31.
3. *Ibid.,* p. 29.
4. *Ibid.,* p. 32.
5. *Ibid.,* pp. 51, 52.

CHAPTER II

Proofs of God's Existence

People who have an epistemological interest in the philosophy of religion often express that interest in the form of a demand for some *proof*—usually of God's existence. Consequently, there have been a large number of attempts to satisfy that demand, along with a similar number of criticisms of such attempts. A disproportionately large part of the philosophy of religion has thus centered around the problem of proof.

This chapter will discuss the possibility of proving God's existence, the conditions that must be fulfilled for this to be done successfully, and the results that we could reasonably expect from such attempts. The discussion, however, is subject to an important restriction. Since it would be tiresome to repeat the restriction continuously, hopefully it can be made clear here. This chapter will be limited to a consideration of one specific method of proof but it is one that has loomed very large in the history of both philosophy and theology. Proofs of this sort may be called *discursive,* since the proof consists of an argument, presented entirely by talking or writing. Ordinary English usage, of course, recognizes other senses of the verb "to prove." A boy scout proves that he knows how to tie knots by actually tying them for the scoutmaster rather than by talking to him and, as mentioned before, the attorney proves his point in court partly by argument but also partly by exhibiting photographs, weapons, and other evidence. A consideration of the theological analogues of these latter types of proof will be left to the discussion of the experience of God in Chapter III. Here we will consider only those proofs that are given *entirely* in the form of argument. Furthermore, the discussion will be restricted to considering deductive, rather than inductive, arguments. But I believe that the substantive points made will apply equally well to inductive attempts. It will not be necessary, however, to repeat continuously the qualifying adjectives discursive and deductive.

Section (1) explores three preliminary questions about the project of proof—questions that partly anticipate some of the succeeding discussion. Section (2) presents an unusually simple argument for God's existence—an argument that is also unusually strong in some ways—and also discusses some criticisms that might be urged against it. Section (3) discusses whether this argument proves God's existence and distinguishes between constructing an argument for p and proving p. Section (4) contains two further attempts to define the notion of a proof, one of which is more satisfactory. Section (5) generalizes a distinction that is implicit in Section (4) and which extends well beyond the area of proof in its importance. Section (6) discusses the limitations of proof and the results that can reasonably be expected from attempts to prove the existence of God.

1 ◆§ *Three Preliminary Questions*

WHAT IS IT WORTH? The first of these three questions is: If it is possible to prove God's existence, would it be worth doing so? We should not be too hasty in giving an affirmative answer to this question. After all, the mere fact that something is possible is not by itself a reason for thinking that it is worthwhile. To commit yourself to doing everything that is possible is almost surely to guarantee that you will do very little that is valuable. Suppose then that I could prove the existence of God and it would take me a year to do it. Would it be worth a year's time? A year's salary? Why? Or why not?

One might reply that God is very important and, therefore, doing anything that is related to Him is very important and worthwhile. I agree that God is very important (although I will not argue for it here), but the argument based on that assumption seems fallacious. The project of proving the existence of God will not inherit any of the importance of God merely by bearing *any* relation to Him; it must be related to Him in an important or worthwhile way. Is it?

Again someone might reply that it would be very worthwhile to know that God exists, and if one *proves* that God exists then people will *know* that God exists. Such a proof, therefore, would be valuable. This is an interesting suggestion and we will come back to it in Section (4) below.

WHAT IF WE FAIL? The second question is: If it should happen that God's existence cannot be proved would that be any cause for regret or disappointment? Again we ought not to rush into an affirmative answer. The mere fact that something cannot be done does not seem to be a just cause for regret. I cannot recall, for example, ever feeling any sorrow over the fact that it is not possible to trisect an angle by

Euclidian means. Of course, if someone has committed himself to this project he may be disappointed to discover that he cannot succeed, but this seems to be more closely related to his special ambition than to the significance of the project itself. Is there some significance in the project of proving God's existence that would make its impossibility disturbing?

Earlier the following proposition was suggested:

(a) If one proved the existence of God, then people would know that God exists.

We have not yet examined (a) very carefully but it seems to have some plausibility and many people would probably accept it. They might also be inclined to derive from it another proposition:

(b) If one does not prove that God exists, then people would not know that God exists.

Now, if (b) were true it would be an important consequence of failing to prove God's existence, and such a failure might well be a cause of regret. Unfortunately, however, (b) does not follow from (a) and so (a), even if it should be true and we should accept it, does not provide us with a reason for accepting (b).*

Of course, if we had some other reason for believing (b), it might still be acceptable and would support the view that a failure to prove God's existence would be significant and perhaps regrettable. In fact, even the weaker

(b″) If one did not prove God's existence then people *probably* would not know that He exists.

---

* Consider for example,
  (a′) If he jumps he will be injured.
from this it does *not* follow that
  (b′) If he does not jump he will not be injured. For he may well be injured whether or not he jumps. Similarly, nothing in (a) preludes the possibility that there may be other ways of knowing about God. Thus (a) does not entail (b).

would support the view. Are there reasons to believe either
(b) or (b″) or any similar proposition? Or is there any other
kind of significance that can be attributed to a failure in
proving God's existence? We will come back to this as well.

MUST WE KNOW IT? The third question is: Is it possible that
someone has proved the existence of God without anyone
(even the man who did the proving) knowing that he had
done so? Perhaps this question seems absurd. But it might
again be best to hesitate a moment before committing ourselves to a negative answer. There are certainly some cases in
which it is possible for a person to do something without
either his or anyone else's knowing that he has done it. For
example, it is possible for a hunter to shoot the largest elephant in Africa without him or anyone else knowing that he
has done so. Such an incident might occur because it is possible for an animal to *be* the largest elephant in Africa without anyone knowing it. But is it also possible for something
to be a proof of God's existence without anyone knowing that
it is? Is it possible for someone to construct such proof (perhaps playfully or by accident) without knowing it himself?
If this is not possible, what is it about a proof that renders
such an event impossible?

If, on the other hand, we suppose that it is possible to
construct such a proof without anyone's knowing it, then we
are brought back to something like the first question: What
would be the significance or importance of that event? Are we
inclined to say that it would have none? But many events can
be important even if no one knows they have occurred. If
the cook inadvertently poisons the banquet, this is likely to be
important, even if neither he nor anyone else knows that it has
been done. (In fact, the guests may die from the effects of
the poison without knowing the cause of their misfortune and
without anyone else knowing it either.) Constructing a proof
may, of course, be much different from poisoning a dinner.
But just what is the important difference that is relevant to
this question?

RECOGNIZING A PROOF. To know (or perhaps to stipulate) answers to these three questions is also to know (or to stipulate) a good deal about what a proof is. The remainder of this chapter is largely a discussion of just this topic. At this point, however, we should take note of an important distinction. Knowing what a proof is may not be quite the same thing as being in a position to recognize a proof, although it may help in such a recognition. For example, I know (in the theoretical sense) what it is to be the oldest man now living in the United States but I am not in a position to recognize reliably such a man. Consequently, I can *understand* the claim that a certain Sioux Indian of North Dakota is the oldest man now living in the United States without being in a position to know whether that claim is *true*. It might, therefore, be possible for a person to know what a proof is while he is unable to determine whether a certain attempt is, in fact, a proof.

2 ◄§ *A Simple Argument for the Existence of God*

THE ARGUMENT STATED. Consider the following argument:

I   (1a) Either nothing exists or God exists.
(1b) Something exists.
(1c) Therefore, God exists.

First, it may be wise to recall that this is not a *proof* of God's existence (that topic is discussed in the following section), but rather an *argument* for the existence of God. It is called an argument for the *existence of God* since "God exists" is its conclusion. In general, an argument will be an argument for *p* if and only if its conclusion is *p*.

The second premise is to be understood in the most prosaic possible sense—that which is entailed by propositions such as "I exist" and "A few eighteenth-century clocks still exist." The first premise is to be understood in its weakest possible sense. The "either . . . or . . ." that occurs in it is to be taken as an inclusive, truth-functional disjunction. That is, the entire statement should be taken to assert merely that one or both of its constituent disjuncts is true, and nothing more. In particular, it should not be taken to assert (or deny) that there is any logical or causal relation between the disjuncts or between the facts or entities to which they refer. It expresses a truth relation only and is noncommittal with respect to other relations. Therefore, it contains *less* information than we might sometimes want to have.*

We will now consider three of the most important sorts of criticism that might be urged against this argument. Some other possible criticisms are discussed in succeeding sections.

IS IT VALID? Rather surprisingly, some professional philosophers, on first hearing this argument, have declared it invalid. (Perhaps they were accustomed to hearing invalid arguments for the existence of God.) Its form, however (a disjunctive syllogism), is such that it is logically impossible for the conclusion to be false if the premises are true. If we adopt this usual definition of *validity* (as I will do), then we must accept this argument as valid.

IS IT SOUND? Let us follow some logicians in defining a *sound* argument as one that is valid and whose premises are all true. A consequence of this definition, when it is combined with that for validity, is that all sound arguments have true conclusions. Furthermore, the soundness of the argument involved may well be at least a necessary condition for a satisfactory proof.

---

* Some readers may find it easier to follow an equivalent account of statements of this form. When the "or" is taken in the inclusive, truth-functional sense, then an expression of the form "*p* or *q*" is totally equivalent to the longer expression: "The following is a list of propositions, at least one of which is true: (1) *p*, (2) q." If anyone prefers this longer form of expression, he may replace (1a) with the corresponding expression of the longer form.

Since we have already seen that argument (I) is valid, the question of its soundness becomes simply a question about the truth of its premises. The second premise (1b), however, seems obvious. At any rate, if anyone doubts it I will not undertake to convince him of its truth. Such a person, however, may still be able to construct for himself an analogue of this argument which will have the same important features. If he knows *any* true proposition, let him substitute it for (1b), and let him substitute its denial for the first disjunct in (1a). The resulting argument will function in the same way as mine.

This brings us to (1a). Is it true? I believe that it is, but I will not argue this point here. Instead, note that (1a) is logically entailed by the proposition "God exists" (which is identical with the conclusion). Consequently, (1a) is true if God exists, and false only if there is no God. This fact has at least three consequences.

First, a person who criticizes this argument as unsound and who also wishes to be consistent must either deny its validity or else deny the truth of (1b)—both of which are implausible and unlikely moves—or else he must adopt an explicitly atheistic position. Agnosticism is not enough for it leaves open the possibility of God's existence and thus provides no basis for the charge of unsoundness here. This is one example of the general truth that criticizing an argument—just like defending one—costs something. It requires some positive commitment on the part of the critic; and, in general, the stronger the criticism the stronger (and riskier) must be that commitment. What has been constructed here is an argument that cannot be strongly rejected (declared unsound) except by a person who is willing to risk a strong and positive stand on the metaphysical and theological question of God.

Incidentally, the commitment required here has an interesting corollary. Some people profess to believe that one should always be ready to defend or prove every statement that he makes. I do not hold this principle, for reasons which may become clearer later on. Those who do hold this principle, however, might be expected to apply it to themselves. Therefore, if any of them are inclined to call this argument unsound they should be prepared not only to adopt but also to prove the atheist position.

The second major consequence related to this corollary is that neither Hume nor Kant nor any other philosopher can have shown or proved that there are no sound arguments for God's existence unless he has also proved that there is no God. So far as I know, neither Hume nor Kant even claimed to prove the latter proposition. It is often claimed, however, that in some way one or both of them dealt theistic argumentation a fatal blow. If that is so, then they must have done it in some way other than by showing there are no sound arguments for God's existence. But it is far from clear what such an alternative might be.

The third consequence is simply that unless argument (I) is sound, no argument for God's existence is sound. There are, no doubt, many arguments for His existence that are far more sophisticated than this one, and some of them may have virtues that this lacks. But none of them can be sound if this one is not. For, as we noted earlier, no argument for God's existence can be sound unless God exists. And if God exists then my argument is sound.

CAN (1a) BE PROVED? Now that we have discussed those criticisms that focus upon the logic of my argument or upon the truth of its premises, let us turn to a somewhat different sort of criticism that will direct our attention toward the defects that this argument may really have. In a preliminary way this criticism charges that (1a), though possibly true, has not been *proved* to be true.

If we restrict the range of this charge to what has been proved in this book, the charge is certainly true. I have not even attempted to prove (1a), let alone succeeded in that task. But though the charge is true, the proper initial response to it is, "So what?" This question must not be misunderstood. It has an important answer and that is the very reason why it should be asked.

We might note as a beginning that (1b) has not been proved either; and, in fact, I specifically declined that task. But hardly anyone is likely to charge that not proving the second premise is a defect in the argument. Why not? Premise (1b) is, after all, just as essential to my argument as (1a). Is it because most people already know (1b)? I suspect that it is. But perhaps some people already know (1a) too. (After all, I claim to know it myself.) But the objector may continue to argue that he does not know it. I am prepared to accept that claim as true also but again I want to ask, "So what? How does the fact that he does not know my premise to be true make my argument defective?" The only plausible reply that comes to mind is that this fact will make my argument useless or ineffective for that objector. This may be true and, if so, it identifies an important defect, provided that the argument is intended to convince that objector.

CAN ONE PROVE ALL HIS PREMISES? Before leaving this general objection, perhaps we ought to explore another variant. Someone may claim, in principle, that any argument for *p* is defective unless all of its premises are proved. (We might call this the "proved-premise" principle.) And since argument (I) does not conform to this principle it is defective. But how shall we understand the term "proved" which occurs in this principle? Suppose, for the moment, that we understand it as requiring merely the construction of some other sound arguments that have these premises as conclusions.

At this point a further question arises. It is quite possible to construct a series of sound arguments such that the first one has a premise *p* and a conclusion *q*, the second one has *q* for a premise and *r* for a conclusion, and so on until there is one that has *z* for a premise and *p* for its conclusion. We might call this circular chain of argumentation. Supposing that all the arguments in this circle are sound, would the construction of such a circle satisfy the proved-premise principle? If the answer is affirmative, then whatever defect my argument may have along this line can be easily remedied. For (1c) directly entails both (1a) and (1b). The circle can therefore be closed by the construction of a single additional argument embodying this entailment. If anyone believes that there is any benefit to be gained from such a circle, he is free to construct it.

Suppose, however, that such circular chains are rejected as satisfying the proved-premise principle. In that case it will not be possible to satisfy that principle for my argument. But this will not be a special defect of my argument for there will be no argument whatever, theological or otherwise, for which that principle can be satisfied. The reason that no argument could satisfy this requirement is that the proved-premise principle (if circular chains are rejected) demands the construction of an infinite series of arguments, each one of which embodies a proof of the premises of the succeeding argument. But since neither I nor any other philosopher can construct an infinite series of arguments, no argument will satisfy this principle.

PROVING SOME PREMISES. The proved-premise principle, which is a universal generalization (and, as we have seen, a self-stultifying or illegitimate one), must not be confused with the demand *in some particular case* for a proof of a certain premise. This latter sort of demand arises in many discussions and need not be stultifying or illegitimate. It will be legitimate if some termination rule for such demands is at least implicitly recognized by the discussants. Such a rule may be formulated something like this: The series of challenges and replies will end when a proof is obtained whose soundness is know to the participants in the discussion. When people use the processes of argument and proof for the sake of extending their own or someone else's knowledge of some subject matter, rather than as mere logical exercises or as demonstrations of technical virtuosity, then they do not demand proofs of what they already know to be true. Under such circumstances the construction of regressive proofs can have a goal that is logically possible to reach and to recognize when it is reached. A man who undertakes the task of supporting a certain argument under this rule can have some hope of completing his task successfully. But if there is no willingness to recognize such a rule, then the task is logically impossible.

The termination rule that has been formulated here contains within it a reference to a certain set of persons— the participants in the discussion. Although this set varies from one discussion to another, for any one application of the rule it identifies certain people whose knowledge is relevant and others whose knowledge is not. Because the set of people involved varies from one application to another, the rule does not determine a fixed termination point for any argument. At most it determines a termination point for a certain argument relative to a certain group of people who are considering it. For another group the termination point may be quite different and may be reached much more easily or with much greater difficulty. This variation is due to the fact that different people bring quite different ranges of initial knowledge with them to the consideration of any question.

Even given that the argument under discussion is in fact sound, the rule does not tell us how to construct a satisfactory support for it. The participants in the discussion know that they will have to find premises that all of them know to be true and a form of argument that they all know to be valid. But the fulfilling of these requirements depends entirely on their own perseverance and ingenuity, which, like initial knowledge, varies from group to group. Consequently, the rule provides no guarantee that, even when the argument under consideration is in fact sound, any particular group will be able to reach the termination point that will convince all the participants. Any teacher presenting an introductory course in geometry faces this problem and very few of them surmount it with respect to the entire class. It is also important to realize that in an undertaking of this sort the successes and failures are independent of each other.

3 ∗ *What Is a Proof?*

In the preceding section a special point was made of not calling my argument a proof, though I believe it to be both valid and sound. In discussing the last objection, however, it was tentatively suggested that we might construe "proof" merely in terms of sound argument. We must now examine this question directly.

LOGIC, TRUTH, AND PROOF. Many people seem to think that the notion of proof can be defined satisfactorily purely in terms of logic and truth. But there does not seem to be any more stringent logical requirement than that of validity. Nor is there any more stringent truth requirement than the one included in the notion of soundness. Every sound argument, then, involves the strongest logical tie between its premises and its conclusion (the logical impossibility of the conclusion's being false if the premises are true) and the truth of all the statements involved in it. If proof can be characterized purely in terms of truth and logic, then it seems that a sound argument must be a proof of its conclusion.

If this is so, however, then either my argument is a proof of God's existence or else there is no God and there cannot be a proof of His existence. If we are satisfied with a notion of proof given entirely in terms of truth and logic, than we need search no further for a proof of God's existence.

HOW TO "PROVE" EVERYTHING. This notion of proof has, however, some peculiar consequences. One of them is that it is extremely easy to prove every true proposition. In fact, we can give a general procedure (there will be, of course, indefinitely many general procedures) for constructing proofs and teach it to any reasonably bright fifth-grade child. He will then be as adept at proving as will any expert in the field.

One such simple general procedure, involving the same pattern as my simple argument, is this: To prove any true proposition *q* choose some other true proposition *p* and use it as the second premise. For the first premise construct the proposition *not-p or q*. These two premises will both be true and will validly entail *q*.

It looks as though proof, if it is construed purely in terms of logic and truth, is a project hardly requiring the training of a philosopher, scientist, or theologian.

PROOF WITHOUT KNOWLEDGE. A second peculiar consequence of construing proof in this way is that it will be possible—and indeed easy—to prove something without knowing anything about it either before or after the proof, and without helping anyone else to know anything about it either. For example, suppose that a person is provided with a list of propositions, of which some are true and the others false. (In order to guarantee that some are true and some are false we might make half of them the contradictories of the other half. Anyone can, of course, make up such a list for himself.) Suppose also that he knows nothing about the subject matter involved and has no idea which ones are true. He can nevertheless easily construct an argument of the form described above for each one of these propositions. Some of these arguments—those with the false conclusions— will be unsound (their first premise will be false). But the others will be perfectly sound. According to this interpretation of what a proof is, he will have proved all of the true propositions on his list. It is clear, however, that such a proof neither represents nor contributes to any knowledge of his own and it is quite possible that it contributes to no one else's knowledge either.

If we were to accept this characterization of a proof purely in terms of logic and truth, then the answers to the three questions introduced in Section (1) seem quite straight-forward. Taking them in reverse order, it is clear that if a proof of a given proposition is possible at all then it is also possible without knowledge, as an accident, or in jest. If a proof is not possible, however, this can be only because the proposition involved is not true. That is, we would fail to prove the existence of God only if He did not exist. The metaphysical fact that He did not exist might, of course, be a cause of disappointment; but there would seem to be no reason for any further lament over our inability to prove His existence.

On the other hand, it is clear that we could construct proofs without doing ourselves or anyone else any cognitive good. Although we might, perhaps, think of some other noncognitive benefit that a proof of this sort might confer, the construction of arguments that do nothing more than satisfy the reguirements of logic and truth, while easy, seems hardly worth the time.

4 ⊷ *Cogent and Convincing Arguments*

The consequences discussed in the preceding section seem entirely paradoxical when compared with more ordinary notions of what a proof is and what it achieves. Perhaps the most prominent feature of these notions is the conviction that the discovery or construction of a proof represents some genuine cognitive advance—an epistemic achievement, an event which is internally and necessarily related to some knowledge-gaining project. This section proposes and discusses two attempts at embodying this cognitive feature in a definition. The second one is successful.

COGENCY. Let us introduce a new technical term, analogous to "sound," to be used in the discussion of arguments. Let us say that an argument is *cogent for a certain person N* if and only if (1) It is sound, and (2) N knows it to be sound.*

The reference to soundness in this definition is sufficiently clear but we should say something here about the introduction of a new element—the references to some particular person N. These references relativize the concept being defined in a way that is crucial for everything else that will be said about proving. The technical term that is introduced here is not "cogent" but "cogent for a certain person N." The references to N reflect the fact that "being known to be true" is a person-related and person-variable property of certain statements in just the way that "being a father" is a person-related and person-variable property of some people. No one is a father unless he is the father *of* somebody, and no statement is known to be true unless it is known *by* someone. The fact that a man is the father of someone does not imply that he is the father of everyone, and the fact that the statement is known to someone does not imply that it is known to everyone. Finally, being a father may give a man a certain legitimate authority in the lives of those whose father he is without giving him that authority in everyone's life, and, similarly, being known may give a statement a legitimate effectiveness in the intellectual lives of those to whom it is known without giving it such an effectiveness for those who do not know it.

If knowledge is going to be introduced into the requirements for proving a conclusion, then it seems clear that the proof-generating force of the argument in question must be limited to the persons who are in possession of the requisite knowledge. Imagine, for example, a murder trial that consists of nothing more than the following pair of arguments, presented respectively by the prosecution and the defense.

II (2a) Either the accused did not commit the crime or he should be convicted.

---

* Strictly speaking, the first clause of this definiens is redundant (given our use of "to know").

(2b) The accused committed the crime.
(2c) Therefore, the accused should be convicted.

III (3a) Either the accused did commit the crime or he
           should be acquitted.
(3b) The accused did not commit the crime.
(3c) Therefore, the accused should be acquitted.

As before, one of these arguments must be sound. In addition, however, of the premises labeled (2b) and (3b) the true one is very likely to be known to be true, by the accused at least, and perhaps also by many other people. But it may not be known to the members of the jury. In that case, regardless of whether one of these arguments proves its conclusion to somebody, it could not prove it to the jury. Neither argument extends the jury's knowledge as neither argument gives jurors any grounds upon which to base their verdict.

This example calls to our attention the relevance of the question *"To whom* did you prove it?" as a response to a claim to have proved a certain statement. The proving of a statement is supposed to be an epistemically significant event. But there is no epistemic significance *in vacuo;* some person must be involved. Who it is that is involved may be a crucial consideration for the epistemic significance often varies from person to person. Any satisfactory account of what it means to prove something must make a place for this crucial consideration. My account makes a place for it at this point.

This is not to say, however, that we now have a satisfactory account of what it is to prove a statement to someone. For even a cogent argument may not always suffice to prove its conclusion, even to those for whom it is cogent. As an illustration consider the following argument:

IV (4a) Either Jupiter has no satellite or President Nixon
           is a Republican.
(4b) Jupiter has a satellite.
(4c) Therefore, President Nixon is a Republican.

Most of us know this argument to be valid and its premises to be true. It is therefore cogent for us. Does it also prove to us that Mr. Nixon is a Republican?

The crucial point to be considered here is not that we already knew Mr. Nixon to be a Republican before we heard this argument. It is rather that, at least for most of us, our knowledge of the truth of the first premise rests on our knowledge of the truth of the conclusion. We accept (4a) as a true premise only because we know (4c) and we can infer (4a) from (4c). Most of us do not have an independent way of knowing (4a) to be true (though, as we shall see later, it is not impossible that we should have such a way).

It seems implausible and unprofitable to speak of an argument's proving its conclusion to someone who must derive his knowledge of the truth of its premises from his prior knowledge of the truth of its conclusion. For such an argument neither enables him to know a conclusion that he did not know before, nor does it provide him with any new grounds for a piece of knowledge that he may already have had. We can therefore conclude that cogent arguments are not always sufficient to prove their conclusions, even to those for whom they are cogent.

CONVINCINGNESS. Let us say that an argument is *convincing for N* if and only if (1) it is cogent for *N,* and (2) *N* knows that each of its premises is true without having to infer any of them from its conclusion or from any other statement or statements that he knows only by an inference from that conclusion.

This definition does not preclude convincing arguments for conclusions that are already known, but it does require that the person for whom the argument is to be convincing should know its premises to be true without having to infer them from its conclusion. Such an argument will provide new or additional grounds for his knowledge of a statement that he may have already known on other grounds.

We have now defined a type of argument that is suffi-

ciently strong, in an epistemic sense, for it to bear the
weight of a definition of "proving." We will have proved
a statement to N if and only if we succeed in presenting N
with an argument that is convincing for him. (N may, of
course, be identical with the person who constructs the
argument. We might, that is, extend our own knowledge
by means of a proof.) For if we do this we will have taken
something that N already knows and will have shown him
how to derive some further consequence from it. N will then
have just as good grounds for this further consequence as
he has for his original knowledge. It seems plausible that
providing grounds of this sort for a new cognitive item
represents an epistemic or cognitive advance.

5 ◂§ *The Cassandra Distinction*

This section represents something of an interruption in
the general line of discussion in this chapter.* It is inserted
here, however, because it generalizes a very important, and
often overlooked distinction, which is made in the preceding
section. Sometimes I am inclined to call this the Cassandra
Distinction because unless we are able to make it, we can
neither tell nor understand the story of Cassandra.[1] According
to the tales of the Trojan War, Cassandra was a Trojan
woman to whom the gods gave both a gift and a doom. The
gift was foresight and prophecy, such that everything she
foretold came true. The doom was that no one believed
her. Our comprehension of this story turns upon our being
able to make the distinction between *truth* and *belief* in
such a way that these concepts have at least some indepen-

* Some readers, therefore, may prefer to proceed directly to Section
(6), returning to this section later.

dence from each other. The distinction that we make here is a special case of the one to be discussed more generally in this section.

SUBJECTIVITY. Let us begin by trying to identify roughly a set of concepts called "propositional concepts" (or "propositional terms"). Let us take the letter p to stand for a proposition or statement and the letter S to stand for a set of propositions or statements. Then consider a sentence of the following form: "p (or S) is ————." A propositional term is one that can reasonably fill the blank in such a sentence. In other words, a propositional term is one that can be applied to propositions or to sets of propositions. We can very readily give a fairly long list of propositional terms that would include, for example: known, believed, unknown, doubted, accepted, rejected, questioned, denied, true, false, probable, improbable, possible, necessary, impossible, doubtful, mistaken, proved, disproved, established, refuted, valid, sound, invalid, and unsound. This list is by no means complete, but this need not trouble us since we will not have occasion to discuss all of the propositional terms nor even all of those listed here. What we will attempt to do in this section is to divide this class of propositional terms into two subclasses by means of a general distinction. These two subclasses will consist of subjective and objective concepts, respectively.

There are evidently some propositional concepts that have psychological implications or content. More precisely, there are some propositional concepts ϕ that are related to psychological states or relations ψ in the following way. The statement "p is ϕ" logically entails the statement "There is some person (or group of persons) who is in psychological state ψ (or has psychological attitude ψ) relative to p." A clear example of a propositional concept with psychological implications is "belief." This statement "p is believed" logically entails the statement "There is some person who has the psychological attitude (or is in the psychological state) of belief relative to p." If it is true that a certain proposition is believed, then it must also be true that there is some person or group of persons who has the psychological attitude of belief relative to that proposition. So the entailment described above holds. There are of course, many other propositional concepts for which a similar sort of entailment holds. It may, however, be worth noting here that, in one respect, belief is a somewhat special case. For *belief* is both a propositional concept and a psychological concept. Hence, in this case, ϕ and ψ turn out to be identical. However, the entailment pattern described above does not require ϕ and ψ to be identical but only that they be related in such a way that the entailment holds. Some of the more interesting propositional concepts that include psychological content are not themselves equivalent to any psychological concept but they do fit our entailment pattern.

Let us call any propositional concept that fits this entailment pattern a "subjective concept." It should be noted, of course, that this is a technical and special use of the word "subjective." It has nothing to do, for example, with the presence or absence of passion, with fairness or unfairness, with proof or lack of proof, with bias or with open-mindedness. Instead, we will say that a propositional concept is subjective, if and only if that concept has psychological content in the sense defined above, regardless of what other properties that concept may or may not have. We use the term subjective to remind ourselves that subjective concepts have implications about the state of some psychological *subject*.

OBJECTIVITY. There are, evidently, some other propositional concepts that have no psychological content. That is, the sort of entailment described above does not hold for them. If such concepts are put in place of ϕ, then statements of the form "*p* is ϕ" do not entail any statement about the psychological state of any person or group. Let us call concepts of this type "objective concepts." Important examples of this class of concepts are "truth" and "falsity." The

Cassandra story itself depends upon our understanding that statements may be true even though no one believes them. In fact it is not even necessary for the person who makes the statement to believe it in order for that statement to be true. But, of course, although it is not necessary for a statement to be believed in order for it to be true, it is also not necessary for it to be doubted or rejected in order for it to be true, since many true statements are believed. The mere fact that a given statement is true entails nothing at all about what any person's attitude is toward that statement.

The following line of reasoning may help to further clarify the above. If truth is to be connected essentially with some psychological state or attitude, what might that state or attitude be? The candidate that comes first to mind is belief. Very well, let us try it. Now, if belief is the psychological attitude involved and if the entailment described above is to hold (we may call it the "subjectivity entailment"), then every true statement must be believed by someone or other. But who is it who is supposed to believe them? Is it perhaps me? The claim that "p is true" entails that "I believe p" and would imply that I believe every true statement! But this seems very close to claiming omniscience. Is it, then, supposed to be someone else who believes all the true propositions? That seems hardly more likely. Perhaps then, no one person is supposed to believe all the truths, but the combined beliefs of some group might be thought to exhaust the realm of truth. Again, however, what might this group be? Even if such a group is proposed, we may ask what will happen if one of the members of this group happens to forget some of the truths which he alone believed or what will happen if he dies? Will those propositions suddenly cease to be truths merely because that particular man happens to forget them? Will they become truths again if after two weeks some other member of the group begins to believe them? The absurdity of these questions seems to indicate that the whole project of connecting truth and belief in this way is headed in the wrong direction.

Similar kinds of absurdity will arise no matter what other psychological notion we attempt to substitute here for belief.

At this point someone might object that if there are truths that no one believes, then no one knows what they are and hence they are of no use to us. This may be true, but it is irrelevant at this point. We are discussing the concept of truth not that of knowledge or of utility. The concept of truth is not identical with that of knowledge although it is related to it. It is also distinct from, though related to, utility. To treat them in the same way is simply to destroy the tools that we must use in our thinking.

MIXED CONCEPTS. I have now tried to explain the distinction between subjectivity and objectivity, and I have given one or two examples of terms which fall into each category. From the way in which the distinction has been defined, however, it is clear that every propositional concept will belong either to the subjective or to the objective class. If it has psychological content, it will be subjective. Otherwise, it will be objective. There are some propositional concepts that will have both psychological and nonpsychological content. Let us call these "mixed concepts." From the discussion of the preceding chapter it should be clear that knowledge (as I construe it, at least) is a mixed concept, since it entails both truth and belief. And it is, indeed, one of the more important and interesting members of this class. The concepts of cogency and convincingness as they were defined in the preceding section are also mixed, as is also the notion of a proof. It is, of course, important to remember that while all mixed concepts are subjective, they convey both psychological and nonpsychological information.

Incidentally, the combining of very different sorts of information into a single concept is not at all unusual nor is it confined to propositional concepts or to philosophical terms generally. For example, the concept *bachelor* includes biological information (about the sex of the person), social or legal information (about his marital status), as well as information pertaining to his age (a boy of five cannot be a bachelor).

PERSON-RELATIVITY. Further important differences between subjective and objective concepts follow from the way in which this distinction has been made. Since the subjective concepts include psychological information, we may say that they are "person-relative." Put in another way, we can say that these concepts always invite the question "Who?" Or more precisely: if ϕ is a subjective concept, then a statement of the form "p is ϕ" must be capable of being expanded into some statement of the form "p is ϕ by (for, to, etc.) N" where N designates some person or group. For example, "p is believed" must be capable of being expanded into "p is believed by N" where N names some person. If there is no true statement of the expanded form, then the unexpanded statement is not true either. This is just another way of saying that if there is no one who believes p then p is not believed. Of course, we may not always know how to expand statements that involve subjective terms. That is, we may not know who the relevant persons are but there must be such persons (or at least some generalizations over persons, such as "somebody" or "everybody") or else the psychological content of the subjective concept will be unfulfilled and the unexpanded statement will be false. On the other hand, since objective concepts contain no psychological content, they need not have any internal reference to persons. Thus, they do not invite the question "Who?" in the same way as subjective concepts, and they need not have expansions of the type that we have just discussed.

PERSON-VARIABILITY. Closely related to the person-relativity of subjective concepts is their "person-variablity" not found in objective concepts. In other words, subjective concepts do not have the same type of opposites as do objective concepts. For example, "false" may be taken as the opposite of "true"; to say that "p is false" is logically incompatible with "p is true" (where p stands for the same proposition in both cases). "Believed," however, does not have an opposite with this feature. For example, "*p* is doubted" is compatible with "*p* is believed" (even where *p* is taken to stand for the same proposition in both cases). This is because "*p* is believed" may be expanded into "*p* is believed by *N*" while "*p* is doubted" may be expanded into "*p* is doubted by *M*." If *M* and *N* are different persons, both of these expansions may easily be true. It is not even clear that "*p* is not believed" is incompatible with "*p* is believed," for the former statement might be taken to mean merely that there is *someone* who does not believe *p*. To form a clear contradictory for "*p* is believed" we must make use of some explicit universal generalizations over persons such as "*p* is believed by no one." No such generalizations over persons are necessary to form the contradictories of statements involving only objective concepts.

The preceding section already called attention to the person-relative and person-variable character of proof. But to neglect this sort of relativity and variability in *any* discussion of epistemological questions would be disastrous, for *knowledge* itself, the concept around which all such discussion revolves, essentially involves exactly these characteristics.

6 ⊸§ *Limitations and Expectations*

This section discusses some of the consequences that can be drawn from the considerations advanced in Section (4) and explores a little further the questions of what we might expect and what we might look for in theological proofs.

COULD A PERSON LEARN ALL HE KNOWS FROM PROOFS? A prominent requirement for a proof is that the person for whom the proof is to be effective should already know something relevant. Argumentation then, as a method of proof, is not a substitute for knowledge any more than a hammer is a substitute for lumber or a needle is a substitute for cloth. Like these other tools, the techniques of valid argument are useful only if we are already in possession of something else besides these tools. If we also have lumber, a hammer may be useful in constructing a house but without lumber it is useless. Similarly, if we already have some knowledge, an argument may help us to know something further but if we know nothing to begin with then argument cannot help us. It follows that no one could gain all of his knowledge by means of argument and proof; and from this it follows that if anyone knows anything at all, there must be some means of gaining knowledge other than by proof.

Once we realize this, we will be in a position to take a more realistic attitude toward the significance of proofs for religion and theology. Since there must be some other way of achieving knowledge in general, it is possible that there may be some other way of achieving theological knowledge. Therefore, we need not consider the question of proof as crucial in the theological case unless we discover some special reason for doing so. On the other hand, since proof is one possible method of achieving knowledge in general, it may be one method of achieving theological knowledge. So the question of proof need not be entirely unimportant either.

IS THERE SOMETHING THAT CANNOT BE PROVED TO ANYONE? There are, no doubt, many true propositions that have never been proved to anyone. There are probably also some propositions that are known to someone, or even widely known, that have never been proved to anyone. But is there some true proposition that by its very nature could not be proved to anyone? This question is not very easy to answer. Since, however, someone might think that a proposition about God's existence might be one of the unprovable ones the question should perhaps be discussed.

. If a proposition, though true, is in principle unknowable, it will also be unprovable. I know of no reason to suppose that the truth about God's existence is in principle unknowable. But if someone supposes that it is, then he will also believe it to be unprovable. Perhaps a more interesting supposition, however, is that there may be a proposition— perhaps "God exists"—that is knowable but unprovable. That is, this proposition must be known in some other way. For this supposition to be correct, there must be a certain pair of statements, *q* and *r*, such that both of them are true and can be known to be true but *r* can be known *only* by inferring it from *q*. We will refer to this condition as the "Condition of Cognitive Order" (CCO). To see the function of this condition, consider a true statement *q* that *can* be known by *N* (though, in fact, he *may* not know it) and another true statement *p* that *is* known to *N*. Then the following argument is sound:

V (5a) Not-*p* or *q*
    (5b) *p*
    (5c) $\therefore$ *q*

Since it is possible for *N* to know (5c), it is possible for him to know (5a); and if *N* knows (5a), the argument is cogent for him. In addition, if he knows (5a) independently of his knowledge of (5c), then the argument is convincing for him. It is this last possibility that the Condition of Cognitive Order must preclude if it is to be true that though *q* can be known, no convincing argument for it is possible. That is, it must be the case that (5a), while it is true and can be known, can be known *only* by inferring it from (5c).

It seems very unlikely that the CCO is ever fulfilled. It might be thought, however, that truth-functional disjunction provides a method of constructing such pairs of statements and that the statements (4a) "Either Jupiter has no satellite, or Mr. Nixon is a Republican," and (4c) "Therefore, Mr. Nixon is a Republican," are such a pair. That is, it might be thought that (4a) could be known only by inferring it from (4c), but this is not the case. An examination of the reason why this pair fails to fulfill the CCO will reveal the difficulty of finding any other pair that does fulfill it.

Though it may not be true, let us suppose that the first person to know (4a) must have come to that knowledge on the basis of his knowledge of (4c). Does it follow that everyone else who knows (4a) must have followed the same path? No. One of the most important and far reaching consequences of the human capacity for rational communication is that the individual does not have to recapitulate in his own intellectual life the intellectual history of the race. For example, the greater part of my knowledge about matters of science and history have usually been gained without my repeating the experiments and observations that first brought that knowledge into human possession. Rather I learned these things from people who knew them. Were this not possible, the extension of human knowledge would long ago have reached its limit.

As a matter of fact, most of the people who know that Mr. Nixon is a Republican were told it by news reporters, political analysts, and writers of campaign literature. Since some people might have come to this knowledge by being assured of this fact by a single competent and reliable authority on the contemporary American political scene, it is possible that someone could come to know (4a) by being assured of its truth by just such an authority. It is highly unlikely, of course, that anyone would undertake to communicate (4a), since the kernel of information that it contains can be communicated in a less circuitous way, merely by asserting that Mr. Nixon is a Republican. But we can imagine cases in which it might even be desirable to communicate a statement from which the desired information could be inferred only with the aid of some other statement. Such a stratagem might serve, for example, in lieu of a prearranged code.[2]

What is important for us here, however, is not the likelihood or utility of a person's coming to know (4a) independently of (4c), but rather the *possibility* of it. And the possibility certainly seems open. In fact, a person might come to know (4a) without knowing (4c), and without being immediately able to infer (4c) either, since he might not know enough astronomy to know whether the statement "Jupiter has a satellite," (4b) is true. But having looked that up, he would then be able to infer (4c) and thus to extend his own knowledge on the basis of these two statements. In his case, the more usual ordering of the knowledge of statements (4a) and (4c) would have been reversed, both temporally and logically. Therefore, the CCO would not be fulfilled by statements (4a) and (4c).

This possibility of learning by communication, and perhaps by other means as well, defeats any attempt to show that the CCO holds true for any pair of statements. If this is so, then for any statement that can be known to be true an argument that is convincing for someone can be constructed.

This has an interesting consequence for my initial simple argument for God's existence. Assuming that God exists and that some people know it, that argument will be cogent for these people. Is it possible that it is also convincing for someone? It will probably seem unlikely that this argument will be convincing for any particular person, since it is so hard to imagine anyone coming to know "Either nothing exists or God exists," (1a) other than by inferring it from "Therefore, God exists," (1c). But there seems no way of entirely ruling out that unlikely possibility. So perhaps even the absurdly simple argument with which this chapter began [propositions (1a)–(1c)] has some possibility of functioning as a proof for someone.

IS THERE SOME ARGUMENT THAT WILL PROVE P TO EVERYONE? For there to be such an argument there must be a set of premises that validly entail p and that are known to everyone. I do not know whether there is any such argument for any proposition whatever because I do not know whether there are any propositions that are known to everyone. Moreover, even if there do happen to be some such propositions, it remains quite likely that no further interesting consequences follow from them. For the most plausible candidates for things that everyone knows are extremely simple propositions such as "There is a world" or "Some things change." It does not seem, however, that interesting conclusions are likely to follow from a collection of statements of this type. Even the simple argument for the existence of God discussed earlier contained something more complex—a disjunction. Some such "combining" proposition that provides a means, as it were, for propositions to operate on each other seems to be required if the argument itself is to be more than trivial.* It is much less plausible, however, to suppose that there is some combining proposition that is universally known.[3]

We are, of course, especially interested in whether there is any argument that will prove God's existence to everyone. Such an argument has apparently not yet been invented. If it is to be invented, there must be some set of propositions that everyone knows and that entail, by logical relations that are also known to everyone, that God exists. The invention of such an argument would, of course, be a wonderful thing, just as would be the development of a drug that would cure all diseases. But there is not much reason to believe that either of these is possible.

It is interesting to note, however, that just this project, or some very similar one, is sometimes demanded (or attempted) as a proof of God's existence. For example, a recent (and in many ways admirable) discussion of some theistic arguments begins by saying

> What the natural theologian sets out to do is to show that some of the central beliefs of theism follow deductively or inductively from propositions that are obviously true and accepted by nearly every sane man (e.g. *Some things are in motion*) together with propositions that are self-evident or necessarily true.[4]

It is perhaps significant, however, that the author gives no reason whatever as to *why* the natural theologian should construe his task in terms of these limitations. So far as I can tell, the vast majority of the things that each of us knows are neither necessary truths nor truths "accepted by nearly

---

* Universal generalizations have the requisite combining power.

every sane man." Why, then, should not each of us make use
of his own knowledge, and extend it by argument if he can,
even if it happens not to be universally shared? It would seem
foolish for anyone else to construe another's ignorance as a
limit upon his own intellectual life. Conversely, we should not
make anyone else's ignorance a barrier to whatever advance
we might be able to make. The notion of a proof as construed in Section (4) takes account of the fact that not every
piece of knowledge is universally shared. It also recognizes
that one person's knowledge may properly be used as a basis
upon which some further advance *for that person* can be
built. There is no reason why an advance of that sort should
not be a suitable project for a natural theologian.

IS THERE SOMETHING THAT CAN BE PROVED TO EVERYONE
BY SOME ARGUMENT OR OTHER?   Perhaps there is, though
this also seems somewhat unlikely. If "God exists" were to be
a proposition of this sort then everyone would have to know
something or other (not necessarily the same thing) that entails
that God exists, and each person would also have to know the
requisite logic. Perhaps everyone does know something of
this sort but there is no reason to think so.

THE QUESTION OF PROOF AND THE QUESTION OF GOD.   I
want to close this chapter by drawing attention to the way
in which the epistemological question about proofs is related
to the theological and metaphysical question about the existence of God. If what I have argued above is correct, then
the epistemological question depends upon the metaphysical
one. It is a mistake to suppose that we can answer the
epistemological question prior to answering the other—either
the answers are simultaneous or else the metaphysical reply
comes first. A person who has settled the metaphysical question can settle the question of proof in the same way. If he is
mistaken about God, of course, he will be mistaken in the
same way about the general possibility of theological proofs.
But while the first mistake might well be lamentable, the
second adds nothing substantial to it. A person who has not

settled the question about God, however, cannot settle the general proof question either. And if he tries to do the latter first, then the whole inquiry is liable to be misdirected and distorted.

For this reason it is important for all the participants in a theological inquiry or discussion to remember that proofs and arguments are epistemological tools to be used when and if they can be used. They are not to be prized for their own sakes nor are they the prime subjects of the discussion and dispute. One who finds an argument unconvincing, for whatever reason or even for no reason that he can specify, need not hesitate to say so. He thereby identifies a fatal defect in the argument as it applies to him. The proponent of the argument need not concern himself with defending it. He should ask, rather, whether it can be strengthened to overcome this defect. If it can be strengthened, fine; if not, let it be set aside without discussion. It is a tool that did not work in that particular case. Let him, therefore, cast about for some other tool, whether another argument or some quite different type of approach, might succeed. For the discussants to forget the great question of God while they quibble over some proof would be disastrous. I have discussed the question of proof here in the hope that it can then be transcended in those situations in which the living issues of faith and life come before us.

NOTES

1. See, for example, the play *Agamemnon* by Aeschylus.
2. This possibility was suggested to me by my colleague, Professor Arthur W. Burks.
3. For a discussion of Aristotle's attempt to show that some generalizations are universally known, see George I. Mavrodes, "Aristotle and Non-contradiction," *The Southern Journal of Philosophy*, Vol. 3, No. 3 (Fall 1965), pp. 111–114.
4. Alvin Plantinga, *God and Other Minds* (Ithaca: Cornell University Press, 1967), p. 4.

CHAPTER III

The Experience
of God

The preceding chapter discussed the epistemological significance of argument and proof. One of my conclusions was that if there is any knowledge at all then there must be some source of knowledge other than argumentation. In this chapter I will examine the epistemological significance of the claim that some knowledge, and in particular some theological knowledge, is derived from direct experience. As in the preceding chapter, however, I will not deal in detail with particular historical claims, nor attempt to settle definitely whether any particular claim to have had a religious experience is or is not correct. Rather, I will again be attempting to construct a framework within which the questions of the reality, nature, and will of God can be discussed and thought about when the circumstances are appropriate. But while the framework of the preceding chapter was that of argument and proof, the framework of this chapter will be constructed in terms of experience.

A corollary of this project is the fact that the present chapter is neutral with respect to several types of purported religious experience. It is equally applicable to mystical experience of the classical type (at least insofar as that experience is thought to involve an element of judgment and cognition), to nonmystical encounter with God, and to revelation.

In Section (1) I examine the concept of experience in general, Section (2) introduces the special problem of mediation in experience, and Section (3) continues the discussion of that problem, relating it to the element of judgment. In the latter two sections the discussion is carried on primarily in terms of sense experience of physical objects. In Section (4) the conclusions of the preceding sections are applied to the experience of God.

1 ◂§ The Concept of Experience

EXPERIENCE AND ITS DETERMINATES. In this chapter, the word "experience" will be used in sentences such as "*N* experiences (an) x" and "*N* had an experience of (an) x." The type of experience that is involved is left undetermined in such sentences. In some cases it can be further specified by sentences such as "*N* saw (heard, smelled, etc.) (an) x." Seeing, hearing, and other sensory perceptions may be called "determinates" of the more general "determinable" experience. That is, the statement that one has had an experience of x can be made more precise (further "determined") by the statement that one has seen (or heard, etc.) (an) x. I do not know how many determinates of experience can usefully be distinguished. But, so far as I can see, no part of the discussion of this chapter depends upon coming to a decision on that point.

EXPERIENCE AND ITS OBJECTS. The word "experience" will be used in a sense which requires that the entity said to be experienced must have some existential independence of the experience itself. That is, the replacement for x in the sentences mentioned above must not refer to the sort of thing that is constituted by the experience itself. Therefore, we will not be discussing the concept of experience which appears in "He felt a great sadness," or "He has had no experience of intense pain." On the other hand, "He saw a camel" and "She heard the bells of the cathedral" are cases to which this analysis does apply. For camels and bells are independent of our experience and have an existence of their own, in a way in which sorrows and pains do not. We will be concerned with possible experience of God only in the sense in which God is not purely a psychological entity, like a pain, but an independent entity with His own existence.

In the sense in which these expressions will be used here, a sentence of the form "N experiences (or sees, hears, etc.) (an) x" will entail "(An) x exists." That is we will not use "experience" to refer simply to a psychological state; "experience" also carries with it a reference to the actual existence of its object. And if that object does not exist then no claim to experience such an object is true, regardless of the psychological state involved.

This appears to me to be the way in which the "experience" terminology is usually, though not uniformly, employed in ordinary conversation. Usually the term "experience" is not used merely to express a psychological state. Thus, we would hesitate to say that a hunter saw a grizzly bear if we ourselves were convinced that no bear was there. We would be more comfortable with expressions like "thought he saw," because we take the word "saw" to include a reference not only to the hunter's psychology but also to the bear's existence. Of course, we do say that the habitual drunkard "sees" snakes. And here we refer only to the drunkard's psychology and not to the existence of any snake. But even in such a case the ordinary speaker is likely to mark the experience word in some special way—by putting it in quotes or by giving it a special intonation—to warn us that it does not bear its usual sense.*

EXPERIENCE AND EFFECT. In my sense "*N* experiences (an) *x*" entails "(An) *x* affects *N* in some way." That is, a thing that has no effect upon me is not one of the things that I experience, even if I happen, by an odd coincidence, to have an image of that thing in my mind. It is not easy, however, to say of just what sort the effect must be. The various determinates of experience seem to specify further the allowable modes of effect; but even here considerable variation seems possible. It would be rash, for example, to suppose that hearing requires that one's eardrum be vibrated by atmospheric sound waves.

EXPERIENCE AND JUDGMENT. "I take "*N* experiences (an) *x*" to entail "*N* makes some appropriate judgment." But again, I do not know how to make more precise just how appropriate the judgment must be. It is fairly clear that a man may really see a wolf in the woods, though he takes it to be a dog. It seems, therefore, that the judgment need not be entirely correct. On the other hand, it also seems clear that a man may be in the presence of a wolf and be affected by the wolf, in the sense that light reflected from the wolf stimulates his eye, etc., and yet make no judgment whatever, perhaps because he is preoccupied. In such a case we would probably say that he failed to see the animal at all.

OTHER ELEMENTS OF EXPERIENCE. The entailments mentioned above do not exhaust the concept of experience (for example, the element of judgment is the only psychological element I have so far mentioned). But experiencing a certain object presumably has a certain "feel" about it in addition

* Readers who prefer to use the word "experience" (and its determinates) in a weaker sense than this are, of course, free to do so. In my sentences they can replace my term with its weaker analogue, provided they then add to such sentences the clause, "and (the) *x* exists."

to the judgment that such an object is present or has a certain property. Presumably, different sorts of experience feel different from each other. But I am not able to say much which is useful about these elements, and I think these are not of crucial importance for the topic at hand.

EXPERIENCE AND REVELATION. Especially in theistic religions, that is, religions which construe God as being a person or very much like a person (though He is not, of course, thought to be a *human* person), the notion of "revelation" is likely to be much more prominent than that of religious experience.

The special features of revelation refer primarily to the nature and action of the object involved and, to a lesser extent, to the type of effect produced. Perhaps we can see some of these features if we think of how a human person's *revealing* himself to us differs from our merely *seeing* him. The person who reveals himself must be active—he must *do* something deliberately for the sake of the revelation. His action, intention, and purpose are essential to his being revealed, but these are irrelevant to a person's merely being experienced. He can be seen, for example, as a rock can be seen, with no initiative on his part.

In general, then, a revelation is an experience that is brought about deliberately by its object and, at least in part, for the sake of the knowledge which the experiencing subject is to gain. It is not, therefore, hard to see why theistic religions, like Christianity and Islam, should find greater use for the revelation terminology. If God is as these religions describe Him, then it seems likely that there is no experience of Him that occurs apart from His initiative and purpose; or simply, that every experience of God is a revelation. But it will still remain true that, since revelation is a species of experience, much of what can be said of experience applies also to revelation. I believe that to be so of the remaining discussion.

2 ❧ *Experience and Mediation*

CHISHOLM'S ACCOUNT.   It is convenient to begin our consideration of this topic by looking at some aspects of Professor Roderick Chisholm's penetrating discussion of sense perception. His crucial definitions are as follows:

First, " 'S *perceives x*' means: *x* appears in some way to S." The term "appears" is defined such that " '*x* appears . . . to S' means: (i) as a consequence of *x* being a proper stimulus of S, S senses . . .; and (ii) in sensing . . ., S senses in a way that is functionally dependent upon the stimulus energy produced in S by *x*."[1]

Chisholm lists the various sorts of proper stimuli:

> We may say that *x* is a proper *visual* stimulus for S provided (i) that light transmitted from *x* stimulates a visual receptor of S, and (ii) that this light, after being transmitted from *x* and before reaching the visual receptors of S, is not reflected. When we look at the moon at night our eyes are stimulated by light from the sun; the proper stimulus, however, is the moon and neither the light nor the sun.

> We may say that *x* is a proper *auditory* stimulus for S provided that sound waves transmitted from *x* stimulate an auditory receptor of S. The proper auditory stimulus is thus neither the sound waves nor the medium through which they are transmitted, but the vibrating object that transmits them. The proper olfactory stimuli are odoriferous particles which stimulate the olefactory receptors; those of *taste* are the substances that enter and stimulate the taste buds; and those of *touch* are whatever, by pushing or pulling the skin, stimulates the touch spots. For other types of kinesthetic sensation it is enough, I think to say that any kinesthetic stimulus is a 'proper stimulus.'[2]

Armed with these definitions we can now explain some

of the determinates of "perceive." " 'S *sees* x' means that, as a consequence of *x* being a proper *visual* stimulus of S, S senses in a way that is functionally dependent upon the stimulus energy produced in S by *x*." By mentioning the other sorts of proper stimuli in the definiens similar definitions can be constructed for "hear," "smell," and the other sensory perceptions. Chisholm also suggests that we may want to add to all these definitions the clause "and S takes *x* to have some characteristic."[3] This clause will eliminate those cases in which *x* causes *S* to sense in some way or other but in which *S* does not believe that he is perceiving anything at all.

A DIFFICULTY.   The account of perceiving that is embodied in this set of definitions has a number of interesting facets but it is also inadequate in some ways. By considering it further we may come to a better understanding of some of the aspects that are involved in our experience of the physical world.

Let us begin with Chisholm's notion of proper visual stimuli; for, according to his definition of seeing, these are the only things that can be seen. An object is a proper visual stimulus for me if it transmits light to my eyes and this light stimulates my eyes, provided that this light is not reflected after being transmitted from the object and before entering my eyes. According to this definition, "generators" of light, such as the sun and an electric light bulb, and also "reflectors" of light, such as the moon and my table top, are all possible transmitters of light. For if both generators and reflectors were not considered as transmitters, then the stipulation that the light must not be reflected at any point between the transmitter and the receptor would be misleading. Certainly we commonly speak of being able to see both sorts of things—we can see the sun (a generator) and also the moon (a reflector).

The stipulation that the light must not be reflected after it leaves the transmitter enables us to see not only the sun, but a variety of objects, such as the moon. Though all the natural light that enters our eyes is generated and transmitted by the sun, when the sun's light is reflected, according to Chisholm's definition, we see the object from which it is reflected, instead of the sun itself.

This facet of the definition accomplishes a part of its purpose, but at a price. It enables the lovers to look up and see the moon; but, unfortunately, it prevents the astronomer from looking into the eyepiece of his reflecting telescope and seeing the moon. It likewise prevents the dentist who pokes his mirror into my mouth from seeing my tooth. The submarine commander will no longer be able to see his target by peering into his periscope, and the avid birdwatcher, instead of getting a better view of the skylark by using a pair of binoculars, will thereby be prevented from seeing the bird at all. Furthermore, this definition will always prevent us from seeing light itself. A proper visual stimulus is defined in such a way that it must be an object that transmits light and hence cannot ever be the light itself. But it surely has seemed to me that I have often seen a searchlight beam sweeping across the night sky. These limitations give cause for suspicion that Chisholm's definition of a proper visual stimulus may not be well formulated.

UNUSUAL INTERMEDIATES. Chisholm attempts to deal with the problems that arise because a chain of events stretches between ourselves and the object or event that we claim to perceive. The difficulties we have found in this definition are likewise linked to that same fact. But before we consider this intermediate chain of events in greater detail let us look at a few further examples drawn from the other senses.

Chisholm says that an object is a proper auditory stimulus if it transmits sound waves that stimulate the ear. He introduces no qualification about reflections here. If the term "transmit" is to be construed analogously to the way that we construed it with regard to light, then both generators and reflectors of sound waves will be counted as transmitters. If so, then when my friend shouts to me from the bottom of a mountain canyon, I may not hear him but rather the cliff from which his voice is echoing.

Let us look at some further ramifications of this problem. With regard to hearing, Chisholm suggests that a proper auditory stimulus transmits sound waves which then stimulate the auditory receptors. According to his definition, we hear a certain thing only if there is a train of sound waves that stretches from that thing to our ears. It seems, however, that we often hear things from which no such train of sound waves extends to our ears. Between the object generating the sound waves and our ears there may be large stretches of space through which no revelant sound wave is being propagated; and, in fact, there may be physical conditions (e.g., an absence of matter) that would render impossible the transmission of any sound wave at all.

For example, both parties of a telephone conversation are able to hear each other although there may be many miles between them. The sound waves generated by one speaker's vocal apparatus become inaudible long before they reach the listener—and yet they can hear each other. Something, of course, is transmitted between them. Sound waves are propagated through the space between the speaker's mouth and the mouthpiece of his telephone, electrical impulses are transmitted along wires between the two instruments, and sound waves are again transmitted from the earpiece of the listener's telephone to his ear. What we are interested in here, of course, is the fact that over a large part of this distance it is not sound waves but electrical impulses that are being propagated. It is indeed possible to transmit sound waves along a wire—sometimes children make toy "telephones" which operate on this principle. But in the ordinary commercial instrument no sound wave is propagated along the wire—a fact that can be verified by anyone who will put his ear to the wire and listen. Chisholm's definitions would require us to say that what we hear is the vibrating diaphragm of the telephone earpiece. But this seems to be just as false and objectionable as the suggestion, which he himself wishes to avoid, "that what people perceive are light waves, sound waves, retinal images, parts of the brain, or ways of appearing."[4]

3 ⋖§ *The Role of Judgment*

CAN INTERMEDIATES BE EXPERIENCED? What has been said so far has shown that it is possible to experience things by seeing them, hearing them, etc., even when certain additional or unusual stages are introduced into the chain of causes and effects that stretches from the object perceived to the perceiver. But there is another aspect of this general problem which must also be considered. We remember that according to Chisholm's set of definitions, it would not be possible for the astronomer to see the moon by using his reflecting telescope. Surely Chisholm must suppose that the astronomer is seeing something when he looks into his telescope. However, I do not think it is quite clear whether his theory would require us to say that the astronomer is seeng the image of the moon or the reflector itself. At any rate, I maintained, in contrast with Chisholm, that the astronomer *is* seeing the moon. But surely there are, in addition to the moon, those other two things, the reflector and the image of the moon. Is it not possible to see them? It must be. There is nothing difficult or obscure about seeing a mirror, and technicians who test astronomical reflectors often carefully examine the images that they form. We should not say therefore that the astronomer *could not* be seeing the reflector or the image of the moon, but only that he *might* be (and probably is) seeing the moon itself. And similar observations should be made about hearing and other types of experience.

INPUT ALIGNMENT. Not only is there this multiplicity of objects which are available to be experienced. The experiencing of one of them is related to the experiencing of others in special ways which do not hold in general for the experiencing of different objects.

Let us refer to the stream of energy that impinges on a sense organ at a given time as the "senory input" that is received by that organ at that time. Then the "visual input" will be the energy impinging on the retina of the eye and the "auditory input" will be the energy impinging on the eardrum. We can include in the descriptions of these various inputs whatever characteristics of the energy we may find to be relevant, such as its intensity, the frequency of acoustic waves, or the patterning of light rays.

It is generally the case that seeing two different objects, such as a man and a tree, involves two different visual inputs, which differ in two ways. First, qualitatively. Seeing a man is generally associated with receiving a visual input of light whose frequency is associated with the coloration of a man and whose pattern of rays reflects the shape of a man, while seeing a tree generally involves a visual input of light whose frequency and pattern are appropriate to the color and shape of a tree. Secondly, the visual inputs in the two cases are generally different in their sources. That is, if we trace the stream of energy back from the observer's eye when he is seeing a man and when he is seeing a tree, then, in the two cases, we will generally come upon some different objects as generators or reflectors of the light, or at least we will come upon them in a different order. Therefore, if we know that a person is seeing one of two objects, we can generally determine which one he is seeing by determining which one is the source of his visual input, perhaps by observing the direction in which his eyes are oriented.

While experiencing two objects ordinarily involves these differences in the associated sensory input, the cases with which we were concerned above do not and cannot exhibit such differences. By the use of a reflecting telescope an astronomer may see the moon or an image of the moon. These two things have only a few characteristics in common. Yet there cannot be a visual input associated with the seeing of one of these objects that is different from that associated with seeing the other. No amount of information about the light entering his eye will give us the slightest clue as to which one the astronomer is seeing. And, no matter how far back we trace the visual input that he is receiving, we will come upon exactly the same entities in the same order in both cases.

Apparently then, there is an entity—the moon—which can be seen by means of a visual input which, under some conditions, is not sufficient to allow us to see the different entity—the mirror image of the moon. The image of the moon can also be seen but whenever this is being seen, the visual input is also sufficient to allow us to see the moon itself. Under such circumstances we can say that the image is in total input alignment with the moon. The moon, however, is in partial input alignment with the image—it is only when the moon is seen in a reflector that it involves the same input as the image.

The case of a mirror image of an object is rather special. Not all of the other cases that we considered above will yield total input alignment, even in one direction. Thus the telephone instrument and my friend are in mutual input alignment (auditory) when my friend is using the telephone and it is functioning properly, but under other circumstances it is possible to hear either one of them with an input quite unrelated to the other. It seems to be the fact that a mirror image of the moon is completely dependent for its existence on the moon which makes possible the total input alignment.

WHAT IS EXPERIENCED? When two or more entities are in input alignment it might seem advisable to adopt the rule that whenever one of them is being experienced then all of them are being experienced. If we adopt this rule, then if the astronomer is looking at the moon through his telescope, he must also be seeing the image of the moon, and if the optical technician is examining the image of a star, then he must also be seeing the star. In the same way, if I hear either my friend or the telephone, then I must hear them both, and if I feel either the pebble or the sole of my shoe, I must feel them both. There will then never be any question of making the distinction which, I argued above, could not be made by reference to any differences in sensory input. And it

might be argued that since the person is undoubtedly receiving the sensory input that is appropriate to experiencing all
of these entities, that therefore he is experiencing all of them.

I think that it is probably better, however, not to adopt
that rule even though it would solve some problems, for it
would eliminate a valuable distinction. The fact that the astronomer is receiving the visual input appropriate to seeing the
image does not show that he is actually seeing the image nor
does the fact that the technician is receiving the visual input
appropriate to seeing the star show that he must be seeing the
star. The proof of this is that a person often receives the visual
input appropriate to and sufficient for experiencing some entity
without thereby experiencing anything at all. This is sometimes due to some organic defect, such as nerve damage,
but not always. For example, only the inexperienced micros-
copist closes one eye when using his instrument—the expert
keeps both eyes open but he sees with only one. There is no
lack of visual input into the idle eye. Light reflected from the
table top enters it—exactly the sort of visual input that is
ordinarily sufficient for seeing the table top—yet he does not
see the table top.

If we are willing to admit that there are cases in which
a person receives a sensory input without having the corresponding sensory experience, then there seems little reason
to insist that if he is experiencing anything in conjunction
with a particular sensory input, then he must be experiencing
all those entities to which that input is appropriate. If this
were the case, then a person could experience some entity
without supposing that he is experiencing it and without
mistaking the thing that he is experiencing for something else.

It often enough happens, of course, that a person will
see a thing of a certain sort without knowing or supposing
that he is seeing a thing of that sort. But this is because
he is mistaken about what sort of thing he is seeing. He may
see a man, for example, and yet he may not know that he is
seeing a man because he takes what he is seeing to be a post.
But if he does not mistake the man for something else and he
does not think that he is seeing a man either, then as far as

this situation goes it appears that he just is not seeing anything at all.[5]

In the cases we have been considering it is quite possible
that a person may be seeing the moon without thinking that
he is seeing an image of the moon. He may, for example, not
know that there is a mirror involved. And he is not mistaking
the image for the moon, for he is seeing the moon itself, not
something else that he mistakes for the moon. It appears
obvious that he is not mistaking that image for something
other than the moon, for he may not suppose that he is seeing
anything else but the moon. So apparently he is neither supposing that he sees the image nor is he mistaking the image
for anything else. Thus, as in the case above, he is not seeing
anything relevant at all; that is, he is not seeing the image.

It is important to distinguish experiencing a thing from
receiving some sort of input from that thing, being affected
by that thing, or even responding (in a broad sense) to that
thing. Experiencing something is a cognitive activity involving
a conscious judgment. The judgment may be mistaken without thereby precluding the experience with which it is associated, but if there is no judgment at all then there is no experience. There is at most effect or response. And in cases of
input alignment it is the judgment which the experiencing
subject makes that determines which of the aligned objects is
actually being apprehended at that time.

EXPERIENCE, MEDIATION, AND ERROR. It is important for
our purposes that we should distinguish different sorts of errors of judgment that may be committed in these contexts,
and that we should discover where the error is in each case.
A person who looks at a man and believes that he is seeing
a post is making what I call an error of perceptual judgment.
A man who looks up at the sky at night and, for some strange
reason, believes that he is seeing images projected on a plane-
tarium dome is also making an error of perceptual judgment.
And so is the desert traveler who suffers a hallucination and
believes that he is seeing an oasis with trees and water. In
none of these cases does the person see what he thinks he

sees, for no such thing is associated with the input he is receiving—there is no relevant post, projected image, or desert oasis.

In the first case it is evident to us that the person is seeing a man instead of a post. In the second case the person described is seeing stars, though he is mistaking them not for other physical objects but for images. We may be more hesitant about saying what the third person is seeing, but it seems that he is seeing what have sometimes been called "sense data" or "appearances" and mistaking them for trees.

On the other hand, a person who looks into a reflecting telescope and thinks that he sees the moon is not making an error of perceptual judgment nor, indeed, any error at all. But we must not overlook the fact that the person who looks into the telescope and thinks that he is seeing an image is not making an error either. There is no good reason to suppose that either of them is not seeing just what he thinks he is seeing. For in these cases, in contrast with those above, there is an entity such as the percipient thinks he is seeing and it is associated with the input he is receiving. The possibility of their seeing two such different things as an astronomical, physical body and a mirror image is due to the fact that the two things are related in a special way—that of input alignment.

Although the persons who make these sorts of perceptual judgments under these circumstances are not mistaken, there is another sort of mistake that they might be prone to make. If the person who is seeing the moon should believe that there is no mirror image involved or that no one in his position could be seeing such an image, then he would be making a mistake. And if the man who is seeing the image should believe that there is no moon (an astronomical, physical body), or that the image which he sees is not dependent on the moon, or that no one who is in his position could be seeing the moon, then he would be making an error. These errors do not consist of mistaking what is experienced for something else. They consist rather of mistaking the relations between what is experienced and other things that are involved in the experience, things that may themselves pass without being experienced. Let us call these mistakes referential errors.

It is not only by denials that referential errors are made. A person who looks up at the sky, sees the stars, and believes that he is seeing them but who also believes that there is a mirror image involved or that someone in his position could see such an image is making just such a mistake. He is not mistaking the stars for anything else, such as an image, but he is mistaking the relations in which he supposes them to stand.

In this connection too, we must not fail to remember that making an erroneous judgment is not the same thing as failing to make a correct judgment. Strictly speaking, the latter is, in itself, not a mistake at all. The man who has no idea at all about the capital of Russia does not thereby make a mistake about Russia, although he does not believe that Moscow is its capital. He simply does not know as much about Russia as he might. His situation must be distinguished from that of the man who believes that Moscow is not the capital of Russia. For this second man is making an error. He is not merely failing to believe something that is true; he is also believing something that is false.

In the same way, in the case of observers who are using the reflecting telescope to see the moon, we must distinguish between the man who simply fails to believe that there is any mirror image involved (he makes no judgment at all about images) from the man who believes that there is no image involved in his perception. The first man is ignorant of some elements in the train of events and entities through which the moon affects him. The second man is, however, not merely ignorant about some elements in that train. He is making a judgment, and a mistaken one, about one of those elements.

DIRECT EXPERIENCE. We have seen that experiencing an object depends partially on the experiencer's receiving an input from that object and partially on the judgment which the experiencer makes in response to that input. We have already seen that the energy stream which constitutes the input may not have its source in the experienced object and that, in its passage from that object to the experiencing subject, it may be involved with a variety of other objects and events. It is a corollary of this that the "directness" of direct experience does not consist in the absence of such a causal train between what is experienced and the one who experiences it. Or at any rate, if it does consist in this, then sense perception of physical objects will not be an instance of direct experience.

It is possible to give another and more applicable interpretation of the notion of directness. The directness of a direct experience is a psychological directness, the immediacy of such an experience is a psychological immediacy. The directness and immediacy do not belong to the process through which the experienced object affects the experiencer. There is no need of directness or immediacy here, and the search for it in this context resembles the project of peeling an onion. It pushes us back from the object to the surface of the object, to the light waves, to the retinal image, to the impulses in the optic nerve, to the brain states. And generally the farther back we are pushed the less plausible becomes the suggestion that this is what we really experience.

EXPERIENCE AND INFERENCE. The immediacy of experience can be contrasted more properly with the mediacy of inference. There are two ways, for example, in which a railroad dispatcher sitting in his office can come to know about a freight train being assembled in the yard by looking at a closed-circuit television receiver. It is possible that he sees the television picture and from that *infers* the existence and properties of the train. He may reason that no such pictures would appear if there were not corresponding physical objects moving in the switching yard. In such a case he would not be seeing or otherwise experiencing the train. He would, indeed, be finding out about it and an essential element in his finding out about it would be his having a certain experience. But another essential element in his finding out about the train is his inference from what he experiences (the television picture) to the existence and properties of something else (the train).

It would, however, be somewhat surprising if a person who was accustomed to using television in work of this sort were to proceed in this way. It is much more probable that, with no inference whatever, his judgment and thought would be directly concerned with the train, and would make no reference whatever to television pictures, to electronic equipment, or to the relations between them and trains. It is the directness of his thought and judgment that distinguishes what happens in this latter case from the former inferential case.

It will often be the case when a certain entity *O* is being experienced that, with the same input, it would be possible to experience a different entity from whose existence or properties it would be possible to infer the existence or the properties of *O*. It will sometimes be the case that when the existence or properties of a certain entity *O* are being inferred from some other entity which is being experienced that it would be possible, with the same input, to experience *O* instead. However, it would be a mistake to suppose that because an entity could be experienced that those who have come to know about it *must* have experienced it. And it would also be a mistake to reason from the fact that the existence or properties of an entity *can* be inferred to the conclusion that those who have come to know about it *must* have done so by making inferences about it.

4 ◄§ Religious Experience

MEDIATION AND RELIGIOUS EXPERIENCE. So far our discussion of experience has proceeded without reference to God or to any other specifically religious concern. The reason for proceeding in this way is that it seemed convenient first to establish the role of both mediation and judgment in experience, and to explore some of the problems associated with them, before introducing any of the special problems associated with religious experience. But now, with this groundwork already laid, we can turn to the special topic of religious experience.

It has often been noted that many reports of putative religious experience associate particular experiences of this sort with a variety of mundane objects or events. It is natural to use "mediation" and similar terms in describing such putative experiences. William E. Hocking, for example says,

> To judge from the history of religions, God has been known for the most part in connection with other objects; not so much separately, if ever separately, as in relation to things and events which have served as media or *mediators* for the divine presence.

> Not everywhere in Nature, but at special points, well-known and numerous enough, the awareness of God seems, as it were, to have broken through, or to have *supervened upon* our ordinary physical experience of those objects.[6]

For illustrative purposes it may be useful to have at hand a brief account of an experience in which the element of mediation is prominent and straightforward. The following report was given by a man who is not a professional preacher, theologian, or philosopher:

> We may hear the voice of God in a biblical passage which comes home to us personally, in the remembrance of a remark made by a friend, in a question which we put to ourselves, in a thought which comes to us when in his presence, sometimes when we least expect it.

> I always remember one New Year's Eve. I had left my wife at home in order to spend the moment of midnight, in accordance with tradition, standing in the Cathedral square with the uncle who had brought me up. When I got back I found my wife overwhelmed and transformed.

"I have suddenly realized for the first time the greatness of God!" she told me.

As the bells rang out, telling of the inexorable and endless march of time, it had been borne in upon her that God was infinitely greater than she had ever imagined. The voice of God had spoken to her through the voice of the bells, and she had answered. Her answer could be read in her radiant face. It was a reply so clear and true that I in my turn was touched by it.

The greatest event in life had taken place: the personal encounter of Creator and creature, the dialogue between the voice of God, so great that it makes itself heard in every earthly sound, without any one of them ever sufficing completely to express it, and the voice of man, so weak that nothing he can say is adequate to the reply. It is an incredible dialogue, so disproportionate are the participants—and yet they are like, for God willed man to be "in his image" (Gen. 1:27); they are both persons, capable of engaging together in dialogue.

We were very weary, my wife and I, at the time. For years I had devoted myself energetically to church work, where as everyone knows, one is always coming up against problems which seem trivial indeed compared with the task to be accomplished. And now, of a sudden, God was showing us his greatness, calling us out of the tangle of sterile arguments in which I had let myself be caught. During the year that followed he led us from experience to experience, to a renewing of our whole personal and professional life, calling us from ecclesiastical activity to a spiritual ministry.[7]

No doubt some readers will not be inclined to accept this account at face value and I will discuss some possible approaches to the question of its veridicality very shortly. But at this point we should merely notice how part of the previous analysis applies to it, assuming that this experience is veridical. Much of the application is not difficult, if the world has those relations to God that are commonly attributed to it by Christian theologians. A woman is sitting at home, apparently listening to the Cathedral bells on New Year's

Eve. She is affected by a sensory input. If we were to trace this input back into the world, we would come upon various entities, such as a vibrating windowpane, the sound waves in the atmosphere, or the vibrating bell. But if we trace the input back to its original source, then, if the theologians are correct, we will come upon God. And God is present in the input of this experience not merely in the distant past but also in the present. At all temporal points of the bell's existence it rests upon the sustaining activity of God. The dependence of the bell upon God is even closer than the dependence of the sound wave upon the bell.[8]

If as a result of receiving this input, the woman thinks directly of neither the sounds nor the bell but rather of God, then why should we not say that she is experiencing God? In this situation, God is being known in conjunction with some other object that serves as a mediator of His presence; that is, an experience of God is supervening upon the experience of some physical object. The language of mediation is particularly appropriate here.

What we have said about the relation of the world to God has been quite general. Consequently, there will not be any object or event in the natural world that could not serve as the mediator of an experience of God. It is no doubt true, as Hocking says, that men have generally found the experience of God in conjunction with certain objects and events rather than in conjunction with all of them indiscriminately. There are probably complex reasons for this selectivity— reasons that may be partly psychological and partly historical. Any object or event, however, *does* have the relationship to God that would make possible its functioning as a mediator. In the terminology introduced earlier, all of the parts of the natural world are in total input alignment with God.

It follows that whenever anyone is experiencing anything he *might* be experiencing God. It would, however, be a mistake to conclude that whenever anyone is experiencing anything he *is* experiencing God. For there are plenty of other things quite distinct from God that he might be experiencing.

There is no more reason to say that every experience is an experience of God than there is to say that a person is always having all the experiences that he might be having. We could, of course, adopt this way of speaking but then we should have to invent some other way of describing what we now describe by the expression "having an experience of *x*." I conclude, therefore, that there is no situation in which a genuine experience of God is precluded, but that it would be wrong to suppose that in every situation everyone is having such an experience.

RELIGIOUS EXPERIENCE AND THEOLOGICAL ARGUMENTATION. If a person is not experiencing God, then is he perhaps experiencing something else from which the existence of God could be inferred? If he is not in a position to assert the existence of God on the grounds of his direct experience, is he perhaps in a position to produce an argument for God's existence on the basis of his experience? To answer this we must ask what sort of thing other than God he is experiencing. Perhaps he is seeing a physical object, a part of the natural world such as a tree. This tree will have a number of different properties and characteristics. Some of them may be known to the observer directly through his own experience. He may, for example, be seeing that the tree is green and comparatively tall. The tree will have other characteristics that the observer will not be discovering, at least on this occasion, as matters of direct experience—for example, the age of the tree. The observer may or may not know about these characteristics by some other means.

If Christian theology is correct, one of the characteristics which this tree has is that it is an entity whose existence is continuously dependent on the activity of God. The existence of something with this characteristic is a perfectly reliable sign of the existence of God. The inference that is involved can be formalized in a number of ways. One way which will yield a deductive argument is to abstract one element of the dependence of the tree upon God in the form of a truth-functional material implication—"If this tree exists, then God exists." It would, of course, be a mistake to suppose that this material implication is a statement of the creature-creator relationship that exists between the tree and God. It is a far weaker statement than that. Rather, it is the expression of the truth-functional relationship of statements about the existence of God and of the tree, and this relationship can be considered as an abstracted element in the much fuller relationship of the tree's existential dependence upon God. Nevertheless, this relationship of existential dependence really does contain the truth-functional one, and the truth-functional relation is sufficiently strong to function satisfactorily in the argument I am constructing here. The second premise of this argument is "This tree exists." From these two statements the conclusion, "God exists," follows.

The similarity between this argument and the simple argument for God's existence that I discussed in Chapter II is obvious.* But here we are considering the possibility that the first premise as well as the second one might come to be known directly through experience. I suggest that not only the existence of the tree but also certain of its characteristics, including its contingency, may possibly be discovered by direct experience. There seems to be little doubt that some of the characteristics of things can be directly experienced. Among these are such things as the color, size, shape, position, texture, taste, odor, and movement of objects. Should the list perhaps also include the radical contingency of physical objects—the existential dependence upon God? How could such a question be answered?

Perhaps we could start with an easier question, one to which we may all already know the answer. Suppose that we are asked whether it is possible to experience the movement of physical objects. No doubt most of us would reply that movement is one of those things that we can directly experience under some circumstances. And I think that this reply would certainly be correct. But how did we discover the

---

* The argument reads: Either God exists or nothing exists; Something exists; Therefore, God exists.

answer to this question? It seems clear that our judgment on this matter is derived from the fact that we *do* experience the movement of objects. When the question is set before us we either recall the many occasions on which we have seen or felt the movement of something or else we glance around us to locate a moving object. From the fact that we ourselves have experienced the characteristic of movement, we conclude that it is one that can be experienced.

A question about the possibility of experiencing the contingency and dependence of natural objects can be decided in the same way. If people do, in fact, directly experience this dependency of natural objects and events, then it is a characteristic that is accessible to experience. If no one ever has such experiences, then perhaps this characteristic is not accessible to experience.

It is especially important to remember that questions of this sort are not to be answered by reference to epistemological theory. Rather, the answers to such questions constitute the starting points of epistemological inquiry. Naturally, we will not expect people who do not believe that objects have this characteristic to believe that anyone ever experiences it. They will naturally consider such alleged experiences to be instances of illusion, misinterpretation, or deception. And if we are interested in bringing them to know that the objects and events of the world do have this characteristic, we would be ill advised to attempt to do it by proving that we or some other person did have such experiences. It would be more to the point to address ourselves directly to the problem of convincing them that things have this characteristic by whatever methods might be suitable for this case. The probable relative inaccessibility to them of the fact that someone else has had such an experience makes it an unpromising starting point for a proof. Even if we use some other method, there is no guarantee that we will succeed in convincing them that either the experiences or the characteristics are as we say. But, as we noted earlier in a somewhat different connection, the failure of some persons to have a certain piece of knowledge or a certain experience does not preclude the attainment of both by other persons. It seems, then, that if the world does bear these dependent relations to God, it may be possible to apprehend *through experience* some characteristics of the world upon which a suitable argument for the existence of God can be based.

Persons whose most common religiously oriented experiences are of the type which apprehends the relations of objects and events to God as characteristics of those objects and events can be expected to think most naturally in terms of discursive proofs of God's existence, since their own knowledge tends to have an inferential character. In most cases, however, the primary arguments involved are so simple that it is very likely that anyone who is in possession of the premises has also drawn the conclusion. Consequently, when arguments of this sort are employed to extend someone else's knowledge of the existence of God, the principal interest is likely to center around the possibility of establishing the premises for the person for whom the argument is constructed.

So far as these attempts are made by providing discursive arguments for these premises, they must be considered in the light of the considerations which we discussed in Chapter 2, Section (2). Sometimes, however, the attempt to establish such premises can be interpreted as an attempt on the part of one person to lead another person into an experience similar to his own. Hopefully, this experience will yield to the second person the same knowledge that it yielded to the first. What can we say of such attempts? How can they be made? What are their prospects for success? These questions are discussed below under the topic of the accessibility of religious experience.

CAN RELIGIOUS EXPERIENCE BE VERIFIED? From the definition of "experience" given previously it follows that if a person has an experience of God then God exists. It does not follow, however, that if a person claims to have such an experience then his claim is true. For instance, some people would doubt that Tournier's wife really did hear the voice of God in the sound of the bells. We may, therefore, be inter-

ested in the following general question: Given that a person
claims to have had an experience of God, is it possible for
someone to verify that his claim is true? This question may
be developed in two different though related directions. In the
theoretical direction it may lead us to wonder whether the
alleged experience of God is logically or formally different
from other sorts of experience. In the practical (or, perhaps,
the "existential") direction the question represents the difficulty of working such claims into one's own theological knowledge. I will follow this question in its theoretical direction first,
since some of the conclusions to be reached there are of value
in discussing its practical aspect, which will be covered in the
following section.

As an example of the development of this question in
the theoretical direction, let us examine a recent book by
Charles B. Martin.[9] He argues that if an experience is to be
understood as being the apprehension of some independently
existing object (i.e., the sense in which I understand it here),
then the experience has to be subject to a set of "checking
procedures." But if the experience is to be construed in a
purely psychological sense (a "low-claim" assertion, in Martin's terminology), then such procedures are irrelevant. Thus
he tells us:

> The presence of a piece of blue paper is not to be read off
> from my experience as of a piece of blue paper. Other
> things are relevant: What would a photograph reveal? Can I
> touch it? What do others see? It is only when I admit the
> relevance of such checking procedures that I can lay claim
> to apprehending the paper, and, indeed, the admission of
> the relevance of such procedures is what gives meaning to
> the assertion that I am apprehending the paper. *What I ap-
> prehend is the sort of thing that can be photographed,
> touched, and seen by others.*[10]

Martin suspects, however, that those who claim religious
experience allow for the relevance of no such checking procedures. He suggests that a theologian might continue to rely
upon his own putative religious experience even though all
of his colleagues suddenly began to reject the belief that God

exists and is the object of such experience. "In this matter his experience may be all that ultimately counts for him in establishing his confidence in the truth of his claim about the existence of God." From this he goes on to draw a conclusion as to the meaning of religious experience claims. "It is quite obvious from these examples that the religious statement 'I have direct experience of God' is of a different status from the physical object statement 'I see a star' and shows a distressing similarity to the low-claim assertion 'I seem to see a star.' "[11]

The correctness of Martin's contention is, however, by no means obvious. As a beginning we might note the difficulty of interpreting his claim that "the presence of a piece of blue paper is not to be read off from my experience . . ." Does he mean that I do not know of the presence of a piece of blue paper merely by seeing it but that I know of its presence only if I photograph it, touch it, and get others to see it? If so, then he must also claim that I rarely know of the presence of a piece of blue paper, or of any other physical object, since I rarely feel called on to carry out any of these checking procedures. But there is a difficulty that goes deeper than this counter-intuitive result. Suppose that I do try to photograph the paper. What then? Martin asks, "What would a photograph reveal?" To discover what the photograph reveals I would ordinarily look at it. But if the presence of a piece of blue paper is not to be "read off" from my experience then the presence of a photograph, and *a fortiori* what the photograph reveals, is not to be read off from my experience either. It begins to look as though I must take a photograph of the photograph, and so on. But of course no progress can be made along that line.

The same sort of thing happens if I try to determine "what others see." I send for my friend to look at the paper. Has he come? Ordinarily I could say "Yes, there he stands. I see him." But his presence is not to be read off from my experience either. Perhaps I must have a third man to tell me whether the second has come and the infinite regress appears again. Interpreted in this way, Martin's thesis fails because it converts into a general requirement something that makes sense only as an occasional procedure. In some particular circumstance I may have a doubt about some putative experience, perhaps my apparent seeing of a piece of blue paper. In that case I might resort to photography or to the testimony of friends to resolve my uncertainty. This procedure does not enable me, however, to substitute a "checked" experience for the unchecked variety. It enables me, rather, to substitute one unchecked experience for another. If I do not rely upon my vision of the paper, I do rely upon my vision of the photo, or upon my sense of touch, or upon the accuracy of my hearing when I listen to my friends' report. I can, perhaps, seek a check for any of these that I wish but to look for a check for all of them is self-stultifying. If I cannot rely upon some unchecked experience of my own, I just cannot get anything out of experience and I must give up the empirical route to knowledge. If Martin's claim is to be plausible, then, it must be interpreted in some other way.

The last sentence of the paragraph quoted above suggests that perhaps Martin requires not the actual carrying out of these checks, but only their possibility. If it is not possible to photograph what I see, if it cannot be touched or seen by others, then I do not see a physical piece of paper. And if I do not claim to see something that can be photographed, etc., then I do not claim to see a physical piece of paper. This sounds plausible since a real piece of paper is indeed "the sort of thing that can be photographed, touched, and seen by others." There are, however, a number of facts that we must keep in mind if we are to properly assess the significance of this requirement for the case of religious experience.

First, the *possibility* of something's occurring is perfectly compatible with its not *actually having occurred,* and with its never occurring. For example, the paper on my desk is the sort of thing that can be photographed, though in fact it has not been and probably never will be photographed. If we adopt this interpretation of Martin's requirement, then we must beware of shifting from a demand for possibilities to a demand for actualities. We have already noted the difficulties, even in nontheological cases, which beset a demand that corroboration of this sort should actually be achieved.

Second, we ought to note the epistemic ordering of judgments about these possibilities. In some cases I might know that a certain piece of paper can be photographed because I have actually done so, and I might judge that it is a real piece of paper—not imaginary or hallucinatory—on the basis of this fact. But this is not the invariant or even the common order for judgments of this sort. Right now I am sure that the paper on my desk can be photographed, although in fact it has not been. And I am sure of this because I am already sure that it is real paper and not imaginary. In this case (and in most cases) the judgment about the reality and independence of the experienced object comes first and the judgment about its possibilities is derivative. We must, therefore, not be surprised to find a similar order occurring in cases of religious experience.

This brings us to the third point. There is no reason why a person who claims to have an experience of God may not claim a corresponding set of possibilities for the God whom he experiences. If in some experience a person really does apprehend God then he can of course claim that God *can* be apprehended by others in a similar sort of experience. He may also claim that God *could* reveal Himself in other sorts of experiences. And he may claim that God *could* do other things that would result in clues to the existence and presence of God. All of these claims are couched in the language of possibility, since that is the interpretation we are now considering. In fact, of course, religious people commonly make much stronger claims; they commonly claim that God has actually revealed Himself to many people, in many ways, and has left in the world a great many clues to His presence. With respect to corroborating experience of other sorts, by other people, the status of religious experience is fundamentally similar to, not different from, that of other types of experience.

There is another way in which Martin's thesis might be understood and it leads to some interesting comparisons.

Martin imagined a theologian who continues to rely upon his own experience even though all of his colleagues have given up their belief in God. Perhaps, then, Martin is troubled because he supposes that the corroboration that religious people claim to be possible is actually tried and fails but the religious people do not accept the verdict. It is like the case of a person who thinks he sees a real piece of paper even when photography is actually tried and the resulting photos are blank, when other people look they see nothing, etc. Such a person, Martin might claim, should now give up his claim of a veridical experience, admitting that the paper he thought he saw was imaginary. And the theologian should do the same when his colleagues no longer confirm the veridicality of his experience of God.

This way of treating the nontheological case is, however, not clear. Imagine that my photos of what clearly seems to me to be a piece of paper turn out to show no paper. How is this to be interpreted? Obviously, the first thought is likely to be of some defect in the camera. But let us imagine that all the mechanisms seem to be in working order. I might reason that a real camera will fail to take pictures of imaginary paper, and that this fact accounts for the failure. But it also seems to be true that an imaginary camera will fail to produce pictures of real paper and this fact would also account for the failure. If I know the camera to be real then I have reason to suspect the reality of the paper, but—in just the same way—if I know the paper to be real I have reason to doubt the reality of the camera. And the same considerations apply to the other methods of checking that might appear to fail. The failure of a checking procedure has no significance at all unless we are already prepared to rely upon some judgment about the elements involved in that procedure. In the case of an ordinary sense experience, it is difficult to see how we could rely upon such elements unless we were prepared to take some of our experiences at face value.

In addition to this, there is another factor to be taken into account when we assess the apparent failure of some checking attempt. It is *possible,* we say, for others to see a real piece of paper. Under what conditions will this possibility be realized? The fact is that we do not know just what the sufficient conditions are and so people sometimes fail to see certain physical objects for reasons which we do not know. There are, however, cases that are more fruitful than that of seeing the paper. I claim, for example, to see a timber wolf in Rocky Mountain National Park. My friend hurries to the same spot but sees no wolf. What significance has this failure? Notice that, unlike the paper, the wolf has some initiative in this affair. If the wolf does not want to be seen, then perhaps my friend will see him only if he is more clever than the wolf. Can I show him the wolf? If I cannot persuade him to be quiet, to tread lightly, and to sit patiently, then perhaps I cannot show my friend the wolf. This failure does not show that my claim should be construed as a "low-claim," or that I did not really see the wolf. The world contains many things, and not all of them are as inert as a piece of paper. To demand that the corroboration of every experience should be equally as easy as substantiating the existence of the paper is simply to exhibit a foolish disregard for the relevant facts.

It seems plausible that religious experience will be subject to both of the factors that we have just been discussing. Since we do not know just what conditions are sufficient even for seeing a piece of paper, it would not be surprising if we also did not know what is involved in some person's failure to meet God. Beyond this, however, it seems clear that if Christian theologians are correct then God will be experienced only when He chooses to reveal Himself. The wolf has a little initiative but he will sometimes be outwitted by the careful stalker. God, however, will not be outwitted or compelled. The failure, then, of one person to apprehend God has very little significance against someone else's positive claim. For it is quite possible that the failure stems from the fact that the man is in some way yet unready for that experience, or from the fact that God—for reasons which we may or may not guess—has not yet chosen to reveal Himself to him.

A person would, therefore, be foolish to give an *a priori* guarantee that he will always reject his own putative religious experience if the majority of his colleagues do not accept it.

(For that matter, he would be foolish to give a corresponding guarantee for his nontheological experience.) So there is nothing especially strange about Martin's fictional theologian, but there is nothing especially characteristic about him either. (I.e., the fictional situation is too sketchy for us to tell whether he is "true to life.") For religious people need not, and customarily do not, suppose themselves to be infallible, either in their experiences or otherwise. They may change their minds like other people, and they sometimes (rightly or wrongly) give up what they previously were sure of on the basis of what other people say about their experience. In fact, a comparison of views is common in most genuine religious life and is not restricted to one's contemporaries. A well-formulated religion, such as Christianity, has much material (Bibles, creeds, etc.) against which the believer is urged to check his own experience. A large part of this material is the distillation of the accounts which previous believers have given of their experience. The final judgment that a person makes over the whole range of the experience of his life and of those testimonies that seem to him to have "the ring of truth"[12] is, of course, both subtle and complex. I do not know of any algorithm for such a judgment. But I suppose that the judgment in the end should answer the question: What is it that, in the light of my whole range of experience and thought, makes the best and the fullest sense?

THE ACCESSIBILITY OF RELIGIOUS EXPERIENCE. In the preceding section I said that the question of the verifiability of religious experience might be understood in a practical or existential sense rather than in a purely theoretical sense. That is, a person may be interested in verifying some claim to have had a certain experience simply because that claim involves something important to his own life. Usually the important element concerns the existence, presence, or activity of the putative object of the experience. For example, if someone says that he has noticed termites in my basement I may be very interested in verifying (or dis-verifying) this experience claim, not because I am especially interested in his experience *per se*, but rather because I am interested in the presence of termites in my home. In most cases a person who is interested in verifying someone's claim to have had a religious experience will be interested primarily because of what can be learned of the existence, nature, and will of God from that experience, if it is veridical. This is the sort of interest that I will discuss here.

A second useful distinction exists between a person who seeks to verify his own putative experience and one who seeks to verify the putative experience of someone else. These two people start with quite different data—one of them begins with a genuine or illusory experience, while the other begins with a *report* of a genuine or illusory experience. And, as we noted in Chapter I, a report of an experience is not at all the same as the experience itself. When a witness describes an accident, he may give us information that he obtained by sight but he does not give us his seeing of it. And our belief will rest upon his testimony, while his belief will not. A person who has a real doubt about some putative experience of his own may well tend to discount the corroborative force of his having had another experience of the same sort. But a person who seeks to verify someone else's report may find that some experience of his own is just what he needs. Analogously, if I should see the termites myself I would probably want no further verification. Verifying one's own experience was discussed in the preceding section. Here I shall discuss primarily those attempts that begin with someone else's report.

A person's report that he has had a certain experience is sometimes taken as strong evidence that he has had such an experience and sometimes it is not. We might divide the factors involved in such a judgment into three classes:

(1) The initial probability that we attach to the possibility of such an experience.
(2) The importance we attach to being right in our judgment; that is, what we risk in making such a judgment.
(3) The credibility of the witness, which is itself a composite of many factors such as his moral character, his reputation as an observer, his readiness to act on his own experience, "The look in his eye," etc.

The importance of (2) is not always recognized but it seems clear that it functions in an important way. If a casual acquaintance reports that he has seen a large dog this morning in one of the lecture halls I would probably believe him, since it is not an intrinsically improbable occurrence. But if someone challenged me to bet a thousand dollars on it I might discover some doubt. If a belief seems to involve little risk and little cost we often do not demand a very strong reason. But a person who understands that his adoption of some religious belief would demand a deep change in his life is likely to demand a correspondingly strong reason for that belief.

Although many of the factors involved in (3) are important, I will deal with none of them in detail. One commonly sought type of corroboration that belongs here, however, may be mentioned briefly. Witnesses are often thought to gain in credibility in proportion to their numbers, independence of each other, and agreement with each other in essential points. In a thoughtful and well-balanced essay, C. D. Broad defends these criteria for credibility and argues that religious experience fulfills them to a substantial degree. Readers who are especially interested in this type of verification will find his essay rewarding.[13]

Obviously (1) is of great importance in assessing experience claims. We will not so readily believe a man who claims to have seen the President of the United States in the hallway of this classroom building as we will believe the man who claims to have seen the president of the university there. For many people, claims of religious experience have a low probability because they assign a low probability to the existence of God. If they became convinced of His existence then they might be much more sympathetic to the experience claims. But, as noted earlier, they are likely to be interested in the experience claims only because they are interested in the existence of God. Perhaps they might settle the latter question and thus by-pass the former.

A person who is interested in, but at the same time doubtful of, some experience claim may think of resolving these doubts by seeking such an experience himself. Thus I may go into the basement, flashlight in hand, to look for the traces of termites with my own eyes. By doing so a person seeks a better basis for, and perhaps a change in, the probability he assigns to such an experience. But he also seeks a direct approach to the alleged object of such experience and a direct verification (or perhaps dis-verification) of its existence and action. This search seems peculiarly appropriate to religious matters, for Christianity, at least, has traditionally stressed the possibility of each man's own fellowship and communion with God. Given then that a person is both interested in and doubtful about religious experience, is there anything that can be done to make that experience more accessible to him? As I said before, I know of nothing that is guaranteed but there are a number of interrelated procedures that are often followed in the attempt to enable other people to have experiences similar to our own. And each of these procedures has specific applications to an experience of God.

Probably the procedure that first comes to mind is that of simply placing the other person in circumstances similar to the ones we were in when we had the relevant experience. "You can see it from over here," we say to our friend who complains that he can't see the parade. And we are most likely to say this if we ourselves are seeing it from "over here." We customarily expect that what has worked for us will probably work for other people.

Indeed, a good part of what is said in connection with proofs of the existence of God can be understood as an invitation to "come over here." People who are interested in some form of the argument from design are likely to include in their presentation an extensive description of the structure and functioning of the human eye, an account of the most unbelievable navigational abilities of some migratory birds, or a report of the intricate interrelationships displayed in some ecological niche, or some such things. In many cases they are referring to situations that have forcefully struck them as being examples of God's design, and thus as being clues to God's presence and activity in the world. Naturally, when they wish to talk to other people about His presence and activity they are likely to revert to these things. They call our attention to the situations in which they themselves have most clearly and forcefully seen the design of God. "Look here," they say, "at the human eye, or at the arctic tern, and you will see that they are the workmanship of God." And they pick these things because they have themselves seen that workmanship there.

This procedure is an obvious and natural one but its effectiveness by itself is likely to be overestimated. We have already noted that if the Christian idea of creation is correct, then every entity in the world is dependent upon God for its existence. It seems that it should also be the case that every entity incorporates some design of God, though there is also a doctrine that much, and perhaps all, of what we see around us suffers from a certain distortion introduced by sin. Everyone, then, is engaged with things that have the relations to God upon which some theistic arguments could be based, or the relations which, for that matter, could yield a more direct experience of God. So if anyone seeks to call someone's attention to a special object that is the workmanship of God, he ought not to forget that whatever this person was interested in before was also the workmanship of God. His failure to recognize that workmanship cannot be due to its not being there and, therefore, cannot be remedied solely by directing his attention to a situation in which it is present.

It is true that these theistic features seem to be more evident in some things than in others and it may therefore be worthwhile to call attention to those things in which they are most evident. However, there are many different factors that determine the degree of obviousness of these theistic features. About some of these factors probably little, if anything, is known. And some of the others seem to be person-variable in ways which may lessen our confidence that what is convincing for one person will also be convincing for others.

The second procedure for enabling others to have experiences similar to our own is to tell the person what to look for. A person is more likely to see the man standing among the trees if we tell him that there is a man there than if we merely ask him to look "out there" and to describe what he sees. This procedure has an associated danger. If I simply direct a person's attention to a scene in which there is no man and ask him to look at it, then he might possibly suffer an hallucination or make a misinterpretation and think that he sees a man there. However, if I tell him that there is a man there I will substantially increase the probability of such a mistake. Just as looking for something in particular increases our chances of finding it, so also looking for something in particular increases the chances that we will *mistakenly* think we have found it.

I mention this danger here to call attention to two facts about it. First, it is a danger, not a certainty. We often actually do find what we are looking for, and do not merely mistakenly suppose that we have found it. Second, it is a general danger and not a specifically theological one. It is present whenever we tell people what they should look for or what they can expect to find. And, accustomed as we are to this danger, we generally judge that it can be sufficiently guarded against and is not serious enough to prevent us from using this procedure. If we were afraid of telling students what to look for, our instruction in the natural sciences, for example, would be radically different than it is—in fact the sciences themselves would not have reached anything like their present state of advancement.

A person who is interested in extending our knowledge of God might call our attention to things or events in which he thinks the theistic features are especially prominent without mentioning those features or telling us what he hoped we would discover by attending to these things. But it would be somewhat unusual for him to use the first procedure without the second. In fact, such a way of going about things would probably strike us as stiff and unnatural, to be justified only by some special circumstance. Why, we would wonder, doesn't he come right out and tell us what he has in mind? The first and second procedures are then almost always combined.

The third procedure is somewhat more indirect and also more ambitious than either of the first two. This method consists of providing an extensive conceptual framework which exhibits the meaning of the particular experience, or at least provides a place for it, by integrating it with a large range (ideally, the whole range) of other experiences. Characteristically, the religious man is likely to take a deprecatory attitude toward the isolated experience (or the isolated proof) whose only content is that God exists. Such an experience is a tenuous one, ill-protected against the doubt as to whether it may have been an illusion or a misinterpretation. And even if it should escape this doubt but lead no further, it is likely to appear to the religious man, especially to the Christian, as being of little import. For God, at least if the Christian doctrine of Him is correct, is engaged not merely in existing or even in maintaining the world in its existence. Rather, He is continually active in the world and is constantly impinging on the lives of men, laying on them the most terrible of demands and at the same time offering to them the most wonderful of gifts. If this is the case, then a man's life is a continuous experience of God, or, as it were, a continuous conversation with Him. Thus a man who has heard the first word and nothing else has not progressed very far, and is, in fact, likely to forget even that first word.

Providing a man with a conceptual framework in which he can see his whole life as being lived in the presence of God is analogous to teaching a man to read a strange script. We can give him a key, a sort of Rosetta stone, by telling him the meaning of one particular inscription. If he believes us he can then understand that inscription. But the test of whether he has really learned how to read the script, and also the confirmation that the translation we gave him was accurate, comes when he encounters all the other inscriptions that are scattered through his world. If he cannot read them, then he has not yet learned that language and he is still subject to the doubt that what we gave him may not have been a translation at all, but rather a message quite unrelated to what was written. He may even doubt that any of the inscriptions are linguistic affairs at all. They may, perhaps, consist merely of glacial scratches. But if he finds that he can read the new inscriptions, if they make sense, if, in fact, he can correspond with those who write that language, and communicate with them, then he has learned that language. And every successful communication increases his grasp of it and also his confidence in it.

The theologian also provides us with a sort of key. He sets out for us the terms in which God is dealing with the world, what He is doing in the world, what sort of things we may expect to hear Him saying to us, and by what means we may increase our capacity to understand that language and to enter more thoroughly into that conversation. Thus, he gives us the whole apparatus of theology. He tells us of God, of creation and providence, of freedom and responsibility, of moral demand, sin, guilt, and judgment, of redemption and forgiveness, of the incarnation, of the Bible, Church, and prayer, of tragedy and death, and of eternal life.

It may seem to us a cumbersome apparatus, and in fact, we may not need it all at once. It may also seem singularly ill-supported. But if some part of it makes contact with some element in our experience so that each one illuminates and makes sense of the other, then we will take a new interest in that theology. If it goes beyond this, if it serves to light up broad ranges of our experience so that we begin to see a kind of sense in our lives, then perhaps we will be more than interested. Most important, if the terms and doctrines provide a clue as to how to respond, and if, as we try that response, we find our experience continuing to make sense, then we are likely to say that the key was a true one and that we also have heard God speaking to us.

I mentioned above that it is unlikely that there are people who know the premises out of which a theistic proof could be constructed but who have failed to draw that conclusion from them. If the construction of such a proof is to be effective, then, it will probably be by virtue of its functioning as an exercise in all three of these procedures at once. It serves to call attention to some event or situation in which the theistic elements may be especially prominent or obvious, and it also serves to inform us as to what sort of elements to look for; as well as to provide us with a set of concepts (e.g., God, creation, contingency, etc.) by means of which to bring the experience to consciousness.

However, these concepts, in virtue of their content and of the doctrines associated with them, also remind us that what we are being called on to see in this particular case is related to a new dimension that we are also being called on to recognize in many other situations. The characteristic that we are called on to recognize in the flight of the arctic tern or the intricacies of the mammalian eye is closely related to the characteristic that is also said to belong to situations of moral demand such as recognition of guilt or hunger for further meaning in our lives. It is likely that if we do come to recognize the theistic elements in one of these, we will recognize it in some others simultaneously. It is probably easier to proceed here by large, rather than by small, increments in our experience.

The reintroduction of the topic of proof in the last few paragraphs of this chapter devoted to experience is deliberate. For purposes of an initial analysis it is useful to distinguish inference rather sharply from direct experience. But it seems probable that in only a few cases—and mostly trivial ones— will we find beliefs whose grounds clearly fall into one or another of these categories. For apprehending an experience, inferring from data and premises, and assessing testimony are not mutually distinct and isolated activities in the life of a rational man. We make use of all of them in all of the important endeavors of our cognitive life. Any really significant belief is almost sure to have its roots, good or bad, weak or strong, in many areas of our lives. If the belief has reasons at all, those reasons are likely to form a web woven of experience, inference, and testimony (and perhaps other factors also)—a web whose scope and complexity will tax and perhaps defy our powers of analysis. When we undertake to examine such a belief, then, or to recommend it to others, we must beware of the temptation to analyze the web too simply, and also of the temptation to suppose that another person's web must be just like our own. Even to the extent that we grasp the truth, our reasons must be as different as the patterns of our lives.

NOTES

1. Roderick Chisholm, *Perceiving: A Philosophical Study* (Ithaca: Cornell University Press, 1957), pp. 148, 149.
2. *Ibid.*, p. 144.
3. *Ibid.*, pp. 149, 150.
4. *Ibid.*, p. 150.
5. *Ibid.*
6. William E. Hocking, *The Meaning of God in Human Experience* (New Haven: Yale University Press, 1912), p. 230.
7. Paul Tournier, *The Meaning of Persons,* tr. by Edwin Hudson (New York: Harper and Brothers, 1952), pp. 167, 168.
8. See, e.g., St. Thomas Aquinas, *Summa Theologica,* Part I, Q. XLIV, A. I, and Q. CIV, A. I; John Calvin, *Institutes of the Christian Religion,* tr. by Henry Beveridge (Edinburgh: printed for the Calvin Translation Society, 1845), I, pp. 189–192, 231–239; Augustus H. Strong, *Systematic Theology* (Philadelphia: The Judson Press, 1907), pp. 371–378, 410–414; Charles Hodge, *Systematic Theology* (New York: Scribner, Armstrong, and Co., 1873), I, pp. 553–568, 575–581.
9. Charles B. Martin, *Religious Belief* (Ithaca: Cornell University Press, 1959), especially Chap. 5.
10. *Ibid.*, pp. 87, 88.
11. *Ibid.*, p. 75.
12. See J. B. Phillips, *The Ring of Truth* (New York: The Macmillan Co., 1967).
13. C. D. Broad, *Religion, Philosophy and Psychical Research* (London: Routledge and Kegan Paul Ltd., 1953), pp.190–201.

CHAPTER IV

The Problem of Evil

In the preceding two chapters our discussion was concerned primarily with reasons that might be given in favor of religious belief. In this chapter I want to make some observations on one type of reason that is often given *against* religious belief. Reasons of this type include references to the existence of evil in the world as essential elements in their formulation. While there may be many variations in these formulations, the general line taken is that the occurrence of evil is inconsistent with some set of religious claims, or at least that evil provides a strong probability against such claims.[1] There can be little doubt that from very early times many people have been powerfully affected by this objection to religion.*

* I believe that this objection, at least as it is applied to Christianity, is mistaken. But I will not argue that point here, just as earlier I did not attempt to prove God's existence or to defend any particular claim of religious experience. And my reason is again similar. Such an argument is not likely to prove helpful in an academic or philosophical context without a preliminary discussion of the nature of the objection itself. I hope to provide such a discussion here.

In Section (1) below I discuss the relation of questions about evil to the problem of evil. In Section (2) I discuss the general structure of this problem and the structure that its solution must have.

1 ◄§ *Questions and the Problem of Evil*

QUESTIONS AND THEOLOGICAL CONSEQUENCES. There are several ways in which one may attempt to formulate and develop the problem of evil. In this section we will consider only one such way, the attempt to put the problem in terms of a set of difficult questions about God and evil. Although such attempts often recur, we may take David Hume's questions as a classical example. (This is not to say that he did not also attempt other formulations of the problem.)

Hume begins his discussion of the problem of evil with a series of questions which he says remain "yet unanswered." "Is he willing to prevent evil, but not able? Then is he impotent. Is he able, but not willing? Then is he malevolent. Is he both able and willing? Whence then is evil?"[2] Now, a number of theologians presumably believe that God is both able and willing to prevent evil. Hume's last question "Whence then is evil?" is apparently directed to them.

This question of Hume's can be interpreted in several interesting ways, among them at least the following:

(1) What is the origin or source (either historical or otherwise) of evil?
(2) What is the effective cause of evil?
(3) What is the purpose or justification for evil?
(4) What is the purpose or justification for allowing evil?

At this point, however, I am concerned more with the significance of these questions themselves than with their possible answers. Let us therefore remember that when a genuine question is asked, one possible sincere response to it may be

"I don't know." And let us imagine that the theologians to whom Hume's question is directed make this response. The questions would then, as Hume says, "remain yet unanswered." What important philosophical or theological conclusion could be drawn from this supposed fact?

Unfortunately, from propositions asserting that theologians do not know the origin, cause, purpose, or justification of evil nothing of interest follows about evil itself nor about its cause, justification, or purpose. Consequently, nothing follows about the possible relations of God and evil. What does follow, of course, are propositions about theologians. It does follow, for example, that theologians do not know everything about their own specialty. But this conclusion is, at best, of biographical, psychological, or sociological interest. It has no theological or philosophical consequences.

Of course, we might, however, combine the theologians' ignorance with the principle that if there were any justification for allowing evil then theologians would surely know it. From that combination we could deduce that there is no such justification, and that might indeed be theologically significant. The principle upon which the deduction depends is so implausible, however, that probably not even Hume would care to use it and any theologian who asserted it would be dismissed out of hand. It appears, then, that even if we allow Hume's assumption, i.e., that his questions remain unanswered, no significant theological consequence can be drawn from it.

QUESTIONS AND EPISTEMIC CONSEQUENCES. One might object, however, that even if no theological consequence follows from Hume's assumption that his questions remain unanswered, an epistemic consequence does follow. One might claim that a failure to answer Hume's question ("whence then is evil?") would imply that one is not justified in believing that God is both omnipotent and benevolent. The argument, which we shall call argument A, might run along the following lines. If one does not know what good reason God has for permitting evil, then one is not justified in believing that God has any such good reason. But in order to believe, in the face of the world's evil and pain, that God is omnipotent and benevolent, one must also believe that He has a good reason for allowing the evil to continue. If this latter belief is unjustified, however, so also is the belief in God's power and goodness (along with a belief in His existence). Thus, theologians who cannot answer Hume's question are unjustified in continuing to believe in God's existence, power, and goodness.

This line of argument appears to be valid. Unfortunately, however, its first premise is highly doubtful. Why should it be necessary to know *what* God's good reason is in order to know, or to believe reasonably, that He has a good reason for permitting evil? I am, for example, justified in believing (on the basis of a mathematical argument) that there is a prime number larger than 3.096×10^{19}. I do not know, however, what that prime number is, and the proof that there is one does not provide much help in determining what it is. Thus it seems that I can sometimes know that there is a certain thing, even though I do not know just *what* thing it is. Perhaps theologians do know, then, that God is justified in permitting evil though they do not know just what His good reason is.

Indeed, it is often the case that I have good reason for believing that a certain person has a justification for some action even though I may not know what the justification is. On the basis of my general knowledge of a certain physician's competence and character, I may have reasonable grounds for believing that he is justified in adopting a certain course of treatment. Except in the vaguest terms, however, I am unlikely to know what that justification is. In fact, it seems plausible to suppose that I could not know what that justification was unless I had considerable competence in medicine myself. But if I cannot be expected to know what the justification is in even such commonplace cases as this, it would not seem at all surprising if theologians did not know the detailed justification for God's actions. In fact, we might be a little surprised if they did.

Perhaps, however, a further objection will be made. It may be said that I have considered examples in which we have independent reasons for believing that there is a justification although we may not know what it is. But does the theologian have any such independent reason for believing that God has a justification for allowing evil? If so, what is it? There are at least two ways in which a theologian might respond without damaging his position.

First, the theologian might reply that he has a reason for his belief, *but he does not know what that reason is.* Consequently, of course, he will not be able to tell us what that reason is. This will sound paradoxical to many philosophers but unless we separate the notion of having a reason from that of knowing a reason, every well-founded belief will force us into an infinite regress. For we shall have to know a reason for that belief, and to know a reason for our belief in that reason, and so on. If this regress fails at any point then the whole set of beliefs involved in it, including the original belief which generated it, will be unfounded. We do, in fact, have some well-founded beliefs but we do not have an infinite set of reasons for every such belief. Consequently, we sometimes have a reason for our belief (or we believe reasonably) although we do not know, and therefore cannot say, what our reason is. If this is so then a theologian who sincerely replies that he does not know what his reason is does so without logical damage to his position.

Replying in this way, however, may be disappointing. The fact that he cannot say what his reason is does not guarantee that he has no reason but the fact that he says he has one does not guarantee that he does. If he cannot say what his reason is, we may find it difficult, or perhaps impossible, to decide whether he does in fact have a reason or whether his reason is a good one. In other words, the discussion may end at this point with neither we nor the theologian being able to learn anything further from each other. This limitation is a shadow that hangs over every genuine discussion (regardless of its subject) in which the participants speak out of their own true convictions. There is no *a priori* guarantee that any such discourse can be carried to a resolution of all differences. If some theological discussion should fail in this way, however, the failure would not reflect upon any theological doctrine or belief.

We will now turn to the second sort of response that the theologian might make when asked why he believes that God has a justification for allowing evil. If he accepts the validity of argument A and if he believes in the existence, power, and goodness of God, then he need never be at a loss for a reason for his belief that God is justified in allowing evil. For if argument A is valid so also must be the following: If God is omnipotent and benevolent, then He cannot allow evil unless there is a justification for allowing it. But He obviously does allow it. Consequently, if He is omnipotent and benevolent, then He has a justification for allowing evil. He is benevolent and omnipotent. Therefore, He is justified in allowing evil.

This argument, which we shall call argument B, depends upon the same ‘conceptual connections among the notions of power, goodness, evil, and justification as does argument A. If argument A is valid then argument B is also valid. It seems, then, that if a theologian is challenged on the basis of argument A he can always construct argument B as his reason for believing that God is justified in allowing evil.

We might expect objections to this argument along two different lines. The first accuses the argument of circularity. It may be said that in assuming the existence, power, and goodness of God this argument begs the question, and that it is therefore epistemically useless in providing a reason for the theologian's belief. There is no doubt that argument B, like all arguments, begs *some* questions. That is, it begins with premises. It is not at all clear, however, that it begs *the* question. The immediate question at issue is whether the theologian has a reason for believing that God is justified in allowing evil. The argument nowhere assumes either that God is so justified or that the theologian has such a reason. Instead the argument deduces that God is justified from quite distinct premises and so purports to exhibit the theologian's reason for his belief. It does not, therefore, beg the immediate question at issue.

If argument B were to be incorporated into a more extended argument for the existence or goodness of God, then it might well render the larger argument circular. But it is not, in fact, being put to that use here. Our hypothetical theologian is not proving God's existence; he is merely replying to the charge that his failure to answer Hume's questions shows that his theological beliefs are unfounded. Argument B is therefore not circular in its larger context either and this line of objection to it must fail.

The second line of objection accuses argument B of relying upon false premises. It is clear that the argument does use premises that are not universally accepted, such as those referring to the existence, power, and goodness of God. If any of these premises are false, then argument B does not provide the theologian with a good reason for his belief in its conclusion. If he has no other reason for that belief, then he has no good reason for it at all. But this is not especially relevant to the present context. For I have been arguing not that the theologian has such a reason but that his failure to answer Hume's question does not show that he lacks such a reason.

The objector might, of course, go beyond *asserting* that those premises are false and attempt to *prove* that they are false. If his proof is successful, however, he will have proved that the theologian's beliefs are defective and that either God does not exist or else He is not omnipotent or not good. This would, of course, be an important theological result (one which, to my knowledge, has not been achieved). And it might be used, in a somewhat ironic fashion, to support this version of the problem of evil. It would be ironic because the consequence to which the problem was presumably to lead is here achieved independently in the course of an attempt to formulate the problem. In any case this theological consequence could not be deduced from the theologian's failure to answer Hume's questions. As I argued earlier, that failure has, at most, biographical and psychological consequences, so that this line of objection to argument B, even if it should succeed, would not show that Hume's questions had theological significance.

QUESTIONS AND SOLUTIONS. We seem unable, then, to draw any theologically interesting conclusion from Hume's questions or from the supposition that they are yet unanswered. And it seems obvious that no other set of similar questions is likely to fare better. If the problem of evil is supposed to lead to significant theological consequences, then, it follows that the problem cannot be formulated in terms of such questions or of someone's failure to answer them. To put the problem in terms of a question is simply to allow the theologian the simplest and safest of responses.

A corollary of this is that someone who is interested in solving the problem of evil must not allow himself to be sidetracked into dealing with such questions. They are interesting and they can be dealt with for their own sakes. But if the solver intends to deal with the problem of evil then he should first demand that the problem be put into a form that appears to involve theological consequences.

2 ⤷ The Problem of Evil as an Epistemic Dilemma

LOGIC, TRUTH, AND THE PROBLEM OF EVIL. If the problem of evil cannot be formulated in terms of questions, perhaps it can be developed in terms of propositions and claims about their truth and logic. Many writers who try to press this problem against the claims of theists contend that the fact that there is evil in the world is incompatible with certain qualities which the theists attribute to God or with His exist-ence.* To state this point more formally, there is said to be a logical contradiction involved in a certain set of propo-sitions: one proposition asserts that "evil exists" and the others assert the existence, omniscience, omnipotence, and perfect goodness of God. All of these propositions are be-lieved by many theists. Hence if these propositions are con-tradictory, then these theists believe a contradiction. As a recent writer, J. L. Mackie, puts it, some of the things a theist believes "can be disproved from other beliefs which he also holds."[3]

Some writers also claim that the problem of evil con-sists of, or is constituted by, this alleged contradiction. The problem is therefore said to be one of logic. Mackie, for example, says, "It is a logical problem, the problem of clarify-ing and reconciling a number of beliefs: it is not a scientific problem that might be solved by further observations, or a practical problem that might be solved by a decision or action. These points are obvious. . . ."[4] I believe, however, that this claim is mistaken, regardless of whether or not the con-contradiction that Mackie alleges actually exists. And this mistake leads one into further difficulties when proposed solutions are examined.† It is, in fact, difficult even to be consistent in holding that the problem of evil is a logical problem. It may be instructive to notice what happens when Mackie tries to discuss the problem of evil in these terms.

At the very outset, besides characterizing the problem as one of logic, Mackie has said that it is one of "reconcil-ing a number of beliefs." But what might this latter project be? Since the remainder of Mackie's paper discusses alleged logical contradictions and inconsistencies among propositions, we might guess that the reconciliation required by the prob-

---

* The fact that such a contradiction is *said* to exist does not, of course, entail that it does exist. It does not appear that anyone has yet suc-ceeded in making the alleged contradiction plain. See e.g., Plantinga, *op. cit.*

† As will become clear, the mistake here is analogous to that involved in thinking that proof can be characterized purely in terms of truth and logic.

lem involves such matters. But if so, the appearance of the word "beliefs" in Mackie's statement is peculiar. For logical relations, including logical incompatibility, subsist among propositions *qua* propositions. The question of whether they are also beliefs, i.e., whether they are believed by someone, is totally irrelevant to any question about their logical relations.

However, even if we take this as a minor oversight and replace "beliefs" by "propositions," it is still not clear what it means to "reconcile" a number of propositions to each other. It is possible to reconcile two people who are enemies but that possibility rests upon the fact that people can change their beliefs, attitudes, and judgments without losing their personal identity. But if two propositions are logically incompatible there is no change that will render them consistent and still allow them to be identified as the same propositions that were previously incompatible. If p and q are incompatible while r and s are not, then this fact alone is conclusive evidence that p and q are not the same pair as r and s. And it seems strange to say that we could reconcile p and q by producing r and s.

The matter is further complicated by the fact that Mackie goes on to say that there are "adequate solutions" of the problem which consist simply of "giving up" one or more of the propositions that are supposed to be incompatible. But giving up a proposition, which I suppose means either ceasing to believe it or ceasing to say that you believe it, is not an operation in logic and hence could not constitute the solution of a logical problem. In fact, to solve a problem by giving up a proposition might well be considered solving it "by a decision or an action." But Mackie has previously associated this kind of solution with practical problems in contrast with logical ones. And it is hard to see how a person might be said to have reconciled a number of propositions (or beliefs) merely by giving up some of them.

Mackie also says that if you give up some of these propositions "then the problem of evil will not arise for you." Since practice is essentially person-related it is easy to see how a practical problem may arise for one person and not for another. The second person may simply not be engaged in the practice to which the problem is relevant. But logic is not person-related in this way. Neither contradiction nor any other logical relation arises or subsists *for* someone. Of course, some people are interested in certain logical relations while others are not, but this can hardly be Mackie's point (if it is, it is surely mistaken). For some people are interested in alleged logical incompatibilities even if they do not believe the propositions involved, while others who do believe them may be uninterested in the alleged logical problem.

In Mackie's paper, then, we are faced with a conflict between, on the one hand, the explicit characterization of the problem as logical rather than scientific or practical, and, on the other hand, his implicit recognition of the person-related character of the problem and of the crucial role played by such nonlogical operations as maintaining or abandoning a belief. (It is the implicit recognition that is fruitful for an understanding of the problem and its solution.) More concisely, the fundamental difficulty in supposing that the problem of evil could be constituted by some logical relation (or any combination of logic and truth) is this: If it were so constituted then it would be a logical truth that either there is a problem which it is logically impossible to solve or else there is absolutely no problem at all and hence nothing to solve. For with respect to any set S of propositions, it is a logical truth that S either is or is not consistent. If S is not consistent then, by definition, the specified problem exists but there is nothing which can be done about it which can plausibly be called a solution. If the theistic beliefs are inconsistent this logical relation was not brought into existence by Epicurus, Hume, or Mackie, and it cannot be dissipated by any theologian. As a purely logical relation, it is quite impervious to any sort of action or procedure including the actions of argumentation, analysis, or explanation. On the other hand, if S is consistent, then again by definition, the specified problem simply does not exist. In that case, the most that could be said of theologians who dealt with this topic would be that they had shown that there just wasn't any problem of evil. But anyone who denies that Job, of Biblical fame, and untold thousands like him were faced with the problem of evil cuts himself off entirely from the historic use of this phrase, and also from the real theological significance that the historic problem embodies.

But what is this historic problem? Surely it must be related somehow to the alleged logical inconsistency that figures in these recent treatments. Surely Job went through his mental agony not merely because of the misfortunes which befell him but also because he believed that these misfortunes were incompatible with God's goodness and justice. What is needed is a characterization of the problem that (1) does justice to its reality—in fact, to its overwhelming pressure and insistence for some people in some situations, (2) leaves it an open question, at least until after the substantive questions of logic have been examined, as to whether the problem can be solved, and (3) makes clear the relation of those questions of logic to the other elements of the problem.

THE ROLE OF BELIEF. Among others, Mackie's treatment itself contains a clue as to one element beyond logic which is required for characterizing this problem. This clue consists of the persistent recurrence of the terms "belief," "believe," and their synonyms. These terms are, in fact, indispensable for a satisfactory formulation of the problem of evil (though not of a logical problem, since they are not terms of logic), and Mackie cannot avoid using them. For example, if there were no one who believed the theistic doctrines, or who was inclined to believe them, or who proposed believing them, or something of the sort, then there would be no problem of evil regardless of the logic of that set of propositions. After all, there are an infinite number of other sets of propositions that have the same logical relations (either consistency or inconsistency) as the theistic set. But there is not an infinite set of problems analogous to the problem of evil.

In addition, most of the other things that Mackie says are related to the fact that this problem essentially involves belief. Belief is person-related and person-variable; that is, a proposition is not believed unless there is someone who believes it, and the fact that one person believes it does not imply that someone else believes it. This accounts for the fact that the problem of evil, to which belief is essential, is a problem only for some people and not for others. And it also accounts for the fact that a solution, or something like a solution, can be achieved by giving up a belief.

We might, therefore, be tempted to say that the problem consists of *believing* the theistic set, which is inconsistent. But that does not go far enough. For again if the theistic set is not inconsistent, then there will just not be any problem. Again, the most that theologians could have done would be to show that the problem does not exist.

EPISTEMIC DILEMMAS.   If we think back to some genuine case of a person facing the problem of evil we can perhaps see what more is needed. Job, we remember, was faced with this problem not simply because he believed something about God's goodness and justice but because in addition he also believed that this suffering was somehow incompatible with what was asserted by the theistic doctrines of God's justice, etc. And this latter belief is also essential to this problem. Its peculiar force and quality depend upon the fact that *the person himself* construes his beliefs as being incompatible or, at least, as counting strongly against each other. This tension is characteristic of the problem of evil and of a small number of other stock philosophical problems.* I propose to call problems of this sort "epistemic dilemmas."

We saw earlier that the problem of evil could not be defined as the belief in an inconsistent set of theological doctrines. However, epistemic dilemmas in general, and the problem of evil as a special case, can be defined as the belief in a more extended set of propositions. A person faces an epistemic dilemma if and only if he believes (or is inclined

---

* Besides the problem of evil, the most widely discussed epistemic dilemma is probably the one that involves free will and determinism.

to believe) a set S of propositions (the "core" of the dilemma) plus an additional proposition I_s (the "rider") which is, "S is inconsistent." The larger set, which consists of the core and the rider, is indeed inconsistent; it is logically impossible for all of its members to be true. If I_s is true then S is inconsistent and some of its members are false. But if all the members of S are true then it is consistent and I_s is false. So the larger set is inconsistent and furthermore its inconsistency cannot pass unnoticed by the person who believes it. For a belief (I_s) that a subset (S) of the larger set (S and I_s) is inconsistent is itself an explicit member of the larger set.

If we now stipulate a core T, which consists of a proposition about evil and some propositions about God's existence, power, and goodness, then *a* problem of evil can be defined as the belief in "core" T plus the belief in rider I_t, "T is inconsistent."

There are several things that we should notice about this analysis:

(1) It has no entailments regarding either the truth or the logic of the propositions in the core (T in the case of the problem of evil). Therefore, the analysis is neutral with respect to these points. Some epistemic problems involve genuine inconsistencies and others only apparent ones. One result of this neutrality is that a dilemma can be recognized as a genuine problem before any substantive question of truth or logic is decided. Another is that people who are inclined to decide these questions in opposite ways can still use this analysis as a framework within which to discuss their disagreement without prejudicing their positions from the outset.

(2) Merely believing a false proposition or an inconsistent set does not constitute a dilemma. This point distinguishes these dilemmas from the far more common cases of simple mistakes or inconsistencies.

(3) According to this analysis, one person's belief in a core that someone else takes to be inconsistent constitutes no dilemma for the believer.

(4) Understood in this way, the problem of evil has absolutely no existence or reality apart from the beliefs and puzzlement of some particular person. It does not subsist *in vacuo*, patiently awaiting its solution.

(5) Since the problem of evil is constituted by the pattern of beliefs held by some one person, it follows that one person's having such a problem is logically independent of someone else's having it. In particular, the fact that some people who believe the theistic set face the problem of evil does not entail that every one who believes this set faces that problem. For there may be people who believe that set and who have no inclination at all to suppose it to be inconsistent. And whether they are right or wrong in this they face no epistemic dilemma.

The concept of an epistemic dilemma, and also the concept of the problem of evil, are not strictly propositional concepts in the sense defined in Chapter II. Consequently, we cannot categorize them as subjective in exactly the sense that is defined there. They have, however, the same fundamental features as the subjective concepts discussed there: the features of being person-relative and person-variable. Furthermore, as defined here they have no objective entailments.

SOLUTIONS OF EPISTEMIC DILEMMAS. At this point we can begin to draw some conclusions about alleged solutions to epistemic dilemmas. Since the problem of evil does not exist in abstraction from particular persons, it cannot be solved in abstraction from such persons any more than a physician could cure influenza without curing any particular patient. If the person involved is in the same state after he has received the proposed solution (or cure) than he was in before, then regardless of its logical (or chemical) virtues we should properly call it unsuccessful. Solutions to epistemic dilemmas, like the dilemmas themselves, cannot be characterized solely by logic and truth values. To be epistemically significant a solution must have some effect upon belief. But such effects are logically independent of the truth values and logic involved in the solution itself. That an explanation is correct or that an argument is sound does not guarantee that it will be accepted or believed.

A corollary of this is the conclusion that for any dilemma that is faced by many people, it is very unlikely that there is one solution that will be convincing to all. For people are too diverse in their evaluation of explanations, their ability to follow analyses, and in the sort of proofs which convince them. There may be many satisfactory solutions (for different people); it is not likely that any solution is *the* solution (for everyone). If any one solution works in a substantial number of cases, it is as good as can reasonably be expected; that it does not convince everyone is a minor defect indeed.

So far we have seen that a certain pattern of belief is both necessary and sufficient for the existence of an epistemic dilemma, and that no pattern of truth values and logic is either necessary or sufficient. Since a certain pattern of belief is sufficient to constitute a dilemma such as the problem of evil, it follows that some alteration of belief is necessary for the elimination of such a problem. And from the necessity of a certain pattern of belief, it follows that there is some alteration of belief that is sufficient to eliminate the problem. We have already noted that every solution of a dilemma should result in the elimination of it. But we may not wish to call every such elimination a solution.

To clarify, at least in part, the additional requirements that we might wish to stipulate for a solution of the problem of evil, let us turn to the other main aspect of the structure of dilemmas—their relation to truth and logic. Such an investigation is not opposed to my previous contention that no pattern of logical relations is either necessary or sufficient to constitute a dilemma. For, once constituted by belief, every dilemma involves a core of propositions that have fixed truth values and that sustain some fixed logical relation among themselves. And we may wish to distinguish types of dilemmas by reference to these characteristics which in themselves are neither necessary nor sufficient for dilemmas in general.

For some dilemmas the core will consist of propositions that are in fact logically incompatible, while in others the core will consist of propositions that are only mistakenly believed to be incompatible. Let us call these "hard" and "soft" dilemmas, respectively.* There are clearly questions of what we might call "epistemic propriety" involved in dealing with these two classes of dilemmas. For example, a man who faces a hard dilemma and is then persuaded that no contradiction is involved in the core (that is, he is persuaded that I_8 is false) is no longer facing a dilemma, but he now seems to be worse off than before. For he still believes as many false propositions as before (those which are members of the core), and he is also lacking one of his former true beliefs (that the core is logically inconsistent). But a person who faces a soft dilemma and then is persuaded that the rider is false is epistemically better off for he has merely shed a false belief (that the core is inconsistent) without losing any true ones.

As applied to epistemic problems, the concept of solving seems to be a mixed concept in the sense defined in Chapter II. That is, when we say that a certain problem has been solved, we imply something about the correctness or propriety of what was done. Thus "solve" might not be properly applied to both of the cases mentioned in the preceding paragraph. We can, of course, introduce a special, purely subjective term (carrying no implications about the truth or logic involved), such as "eliminate." Then we could say that in every case in which a certain person ceases to face a certain dilemma, that dilemma has been eliminated for him. Some of these eliminations will involve epistemic gains and others will involve epistemic losses.

We have, however, already noted the usefulness of mixed concepts such as "prove" and "know" since we often

---

* "Hard" and "soft" are objective terms since they refer solely to the logic of the dilemma *cores*. Consequently, they make "hard dilemma" and "soft dilemma" mixed.

want simultaneously to convey information about psychological matters (beliefs, etc.) and about truth and logic. It would probably be useful, then, to retain "solve" as a mixed concept, which will, of course, be person-relative. Let us say therefore, that a certain dilemma is solved for N if and only if N is rightly persuaded that the rider involved in that dilemma is false. But what is meant by "rightly persuaded" in this context?

As a minimum, no one is rightly persuaded to believe any proposition which is false. Whatever lies at the basis of such a persuasion, such as an argument, a piece of alleged evidence, or a putative experience, must involve some defect of truth or logic either internal to it or in the application or interpretation that is made of it. And had the person involved refused to be persuaded he would have been correct. I am not sure whether any other condition is necessary. Someone may want to make some requirement about the method used in the persuading, but it is not easy to see just what that requirement should be. At any rate, it appears that any such additional conditions will, like the one I have here suggested, make reference to the truth and logic involved in the persuasion. If they do, then the consequences which I draw from my condition will apply to them also.

According to my definition of "solve," only soft dilemmas can be solved. There seems, however, to be also a legitimate elimination procedure for hard dilemmas, which we can perhaps call a "resolution." This procedure consists of abandoning enough false propositions to leave a consistent remainder. Illegitimate elimination procedures include abandoning true propositions in dealing with a soft dilemma and the above-mentioned case of being persuaded that a hard dilemma involves no contradiction. In general, we should count as illegitimate any procedure that results in an epistemic loss—the abandonment of a true belief or the acquisition of a false one.

We can turn now to three final comments on the ways in which the special structure of this problem bears upon the construction and evaluation of solutions or resolutions

First, since a solution must satisfy two different sorts
uirements, those of psychological effectiveness in alter-
liefs and those of epistemic propriety involving truth
gic, it may be open to criticism along either of these
In some ways the latter type of criticism, that the
ed solution contains defects of truth or logic, is more
ul and far-reaching than the former and is more inter-
to many philosophers. But it is not without a corre-
ngly increased danger for the critic himself. The danger
from the fact that in order to make such a criticism
tic must leave the comparatively safe ground of talk
belief, perhaps even his own belief, and must com-
nself on questions that go beyond belief. If I observe
meone is as troubled after receiving a given argument
vas before, then we can conclude that it did not solve
oblem of evil for him. And we can conclude this
t committing ourselves on any matter of truth or
nvolved in the problem or the alleged solution. But
nnot conclude that the solution is logically defective
: it rests upon a false assumption without making
commitment. Any criticism that an alleged solution
s some defect of truth or logic runs a new and ex-
risk of being wrong.
e should not always avoid such risks, of course. The
ian who attempts such a solution takes an analogous
he important point is that the critic who makes a
or logic-oriented objection is not in a privileged posi-
e must make as positive and substantive a claim as
ologian. And the *beliefs* of both the theologian and
c are irrelevant to the *truth* of this claim and counter-
In particular, the fact that the critic is unconvinced
theologian counts for no more than the fact that the
ian is unconvinced by the critic. Of course, the theo-
defender is almost uniformly charged with the burden
f, while critics of his views are often thought to have
obligation. But this is merely an accidental feature
urrent state of culture and philosophy; it has no basis
and reason. In particular, if the claim that the prob-

lem of evil involves no real contradiction obligates its proponent to prove this claim, then the claim that the problem does involve a real contradiction should place an analogous obligation on its proponent.

Second, it appears that answering such a question as "Whence then is evil?" is neither necessary nor sufficient for solving the problem of evil. It is not sufficient because answering a question is not sufficient for altering beliefs. We can often answer a person's question truly without his believing the answer that we give him and without any alteration in any other of his relevant beliefs. And so Hume's question may have often been answered truly, both before and after his time, and yet the problem of evil may remain because the answer was not believed. Answering Hume's question is not a necessary condition for solving the problem of evil because an unanswered question need not be either a psychological barrier to, or a logical defect in, the required alteration of beliefs. There is no subject at all in which I suppose that I know the answer to every question. But this does not prevent me from holding, and sometimes altering, beliefs about some aspects of that subject. In this same way there are many people who neither know nor think that they know whence came evil but who, nevertheless, have no inclination to believe the theistic set inconsistent. There seems to be no reason why a person's failure to know the answer to some question about God should preclude his reasonably and rightfully believing some propositions about God that do not profess to be answers to that question. Thus it is quite possible that a person's doubts about the consistency of his theological beliefs could rightly be eliminated without converting him to any particular theory of the origin of evil.

Third, toward the beginning of this section I defined epistemic dilemmas and said that the problem of evil was of this type. But I did not strictly define *the* problem of evil itself. It is unprofitable to do so, for this phrase has long been used to refer to a whole family of problems rather than to a single well-defined problem. With its person-related character it could hardly be otherwise. These problems are all dilemmas that characteristically involve propositions about God's existence, goodness, and power, and the reality of evil. However, they differ to some extent in exactly what propositions about God are involved; they differ more widely in what propositions about evil appears, and also in what additional propositions are involved. For example, every pastor probably knows someone who is not disturbed by the bare fact of evil in the world, nor even by the amount of it, but whose faith is troubled by some particular suffering, perhaps his own, that he thinks God could not have permitted if He loved the world. This seems to be as genuine a form of the problem as any other and it will probably be unaffected by solutions that deal with evil only in general terms. Other forms of this general problem will involve a variety of additional beliefs about the relation of goodness, power, and evil, and perhaps also about such things as the reality and value of free will, etc. Of course, not all of these propositions belong to Christian theology and many of them will be false, but people who believe them are likely to combine them with their theological beliefs, since they take them all to be true.

We then have another reason for not expecting one solution to this problem—there is not one problem, but many. Furthermore, there is no good reason to suppose that these problems must all be of one type, either all hard or all soft. Consequently they may require widely different treatments. It seems to me that a version of the problem of evil whose core consists entirely of propositions belonging to Christian theology is a soft dilemma and a solution is in order. But someone may easily have combined these propositions with another one which produces a really inconsistent set. What is needed here is a resolution, involving the rejection of some false proposition. But the fact that a certain set is inconsistent, while it entails that some member is false, does nothing to identify which member is the false one. This must be determined on some other grounds. It would, of course, be improper to assume from the outset that it must be the theological members of the set which are at fault.

NOTES

1. For readers who are further interested in this topic some excellent discussions of first-level issues are now available. A number of classical and contemporary attempts to formulate and "press" the problem of evil against religious belief can be found in Nelson Pike (ed.), *God and Evil* (Englewood Cliffs: Prentice-Hall, 1964), and an extensive historical survey of approaches to this topic, along with some original analysis, is given by John Hick, *Evil and the God of Love* (New York: Harper and Row, 1966). One of the most penetrating, yet nontechnical, discussions of this topic is that of C. S. Lewis, *The Problem of Pain* (London: Geoffrey Bles 1940). In *A Grief Observed* (New York: The Seabury Press, 1961) the same author records his later reflections on this problem during a time of deep personal sorrow. An excellent, though rather technical, consideration of anti-theological arguments based upon evil is that of Alvin Plantinga, *God and Other Minds* (Ithaca: Cornell University Press, 1967), chap. 5 and 6.
2. David Hume, *Dialogues Concerning Natural Religion,* Part X.
3. J. L. Mackie, "Evil and Omnipotence," *Mind,* Vol. XLIV, no. 254 (1955). Reprinted in Nelson Pike, *op. cit.*
4. Mackie, *op. cit.*

CHAPTER V

Summary

EPISTEMIC ACTIVITIES AS BOTH PERSON-ORIENTED AND CONTENT-ORIENTED. When we consider any epistemic activity, attitude, or disposition*—such as knowing, believing, proving, discovering, solving, or experiencing—it is possible to distinguish the activity as a whole from the subject upon which it is focused. So a man may prove *the existence of God*, believe in *the historicity of the Exodus*, see a *timber wolf*, know *that he is mortal*, or solve *the problem of evil*. If we abstract this content from the epistemic complex, what is left seems to be some internal state, disposition, or activity of a person—his disposition to believe or his construction of a proof, etc. This element is crucial to every epistemic activity. It constitutes the person's apprehension of (or his attempt to apprehend) the subject matter. It is imporant to remember, however, that this residue is purely the result of abstraction, and can have no reality independent of its

---

* In this chapter, the expression "epistemic activity" will also cover dispositions, attitudes, and states.

intentional content. There is no belief that is not a belief in something, no proof that is not a proof of something, no discovery that has no content. The content, on the other hand, is not purely an abstraction. The timber wolf, the historicity of the Exodus, and the existence of God do not depend upon the seeing, proving, or believing in which they may be involved.

Normally, epistemic activities do not have epistemic activities as their content but on some occasions they do. Thus a person may undertake to prove *that he knows something,* he may believe *that someone else has discovered something,* or he may try to solve *the problem of evil.* Much modern philosophy has centered upon epistemology—the examination and discussion of epistemic activities—and this is often assumed to be the proper critical approach to intellectual life. As a consequence many discussions and investigations of substantive issues now rapidly become expanded by the introduction of the related epistemological issues into the discussion. The fact, however, that epistemic activities are both person-oriented and content-oriented renders such discussions especially susceptible to misunderstanding and futility. In the body of this book I have attempted to move *through* such difficulties, rather than retreating from them, by attempting explicitly to isolate and discuss some of the main epistemological issues, with the hope that such discussion may clear the path for a return to the substantive matters of interest.

EPISTEMOLOGICAL DISCUSSION AS INVOLVING BOTH OBJEC-TIVE AND SUBJECTIVE CONCEPTS. The double orientation of epistemic activities is reflected in the fact that a full range of epistemological claims cannot be made without the use of subjective concepts—such as *belief*—and objective concepts —such as of *truth.* In fact, many of the most interesting and important, as well as confusing, epistemological concepts are mixed, involving both subjective and objective elements. Among such concepts are those of *knowledge, proof, experience,* and *solution.* A large part of the confusion engendered by epistemological discussions arises from the failure to recognize the mixed character of crucial epistemological concepts. Consequently, a large part of this book consists of an attempt to analyze and exhibit this feature.

EPISTEMOLOGICAL JUDGMENTS AS PARASITIC. As a consequence of the double orientation of epistemic activities, many judgments about such activities cannot properly be made independently of the corresponding judgments about the related substantive issues. Characteristically, negative judgments about epistemic activities are sometimes possible independently of substantive judgments but positive judgments about such activities are not possible without prior or simultaneous commitments on the substantive issues. Thus, for example, we can judge that one has failed to prove the existence of God to N solely on the ground that N is *not* convinced. We cannot, however, judge that one has succeeded in proving the existence of God to M merely on the ground that M *is* convinced. We must also decide that God does in fact exist.

In addition, most generalizations about epistemic activities and most judgments about the possibility of such activities seem to be largely dependent upon the corresponding substantive judgments. Thus, for example, our answer to questions about whether anyone has ever proved that God exists, or whether it is possible to prove that He exists, will depend almost entirely upon our judgment as to whether there is a God.

EPISTEMOLOGICAL QUESTIONS AS SECONDARY. A consequence of the dependent character of epistemological judgments is that the corresponding questions must be regarded as secondary. A good workman will pay attention to his tools but he will not pay more attention to them than to the work for whose sake the tools exist. In the end we must stop examining and discussing epistemic activities and we must begin to use them and to engage in them. Hopefully, our reasoning and our experience will lead us to the truth. They will do so, however, only if we finally turn our faces outward, away from the reasoning and the experience itself, and toward the truth that we seek to grasp.

Index